PHILOSOPHIES OF WESTERN EDUCATION

PHILOSOPHIES

OF

WESTERN EDUCATION

by

William H. Howick

Professor of Philosophical and Social Foundations
 of Education
Memphis State University
Memphis, Tennessee

Order from

**The Interstate
Printers & Publishers, Inc.**

Danville, Illinois 61832

PREFACE

There was a time when the subject-title, philosophy, included most other fields of academic study. Generally, the teachers of philosophy and their students in ancient Greece dealt with abstract ideas, the philosophy of mathematics, literature, and education, to mention but a few areas. One only has to read from the great Greek philosophers and their biographers for evidence. Most, if not all, of the early and most prominent thinkers had a synthesized view of learning, which placed philosophy and education in close relationship. As a result we may trace the educator's concern for method at least to Socrates, for structure and system to Plato, and to Aristotle for a suggested curriculum. A similar, unified view of the two fields can be seen in the writings of later philosopher-educators such as Immanuel Kant, Johann Herbart and John Dewey. Although the boundaries of human knowledge now have been extended to a point where almost every field of any age is a specialized subject in itself, the close and natural affinity between philosophy and education remains. So when the authorities in either field criticize the historical content of the other it is as if they were faulting their own subject matter.

In a more modern and recent period in Western history, both philosophy and education moved away from their age-old alinement with abstract and metaphysical assumptions. It should be noted that both fields, somewhat hand-in-hand, became analytical and critical in their approach. But time mixed with experience is a great teacher. One authority recently suggested that theorists had "thrown the baby out with the bath," while another declared that we were moving back to "scrubbed and chastened" metaphysical bases. Perhaps the dissolution resulting from the failure to develop a scientific utopia coupled with the confusion of rebellious students asking for real values has precipitated the return to non-mathematical theory.

This volume represents a step in that gradual return of philosophy and education to abstract constructs only tacitly recognized in recent years. It is not a regression to iron-clad systems, logically organized, and admired for their symmetry and beauty, but not their utility. Rather, a more apt description is that this represents a forward step which views abstract theory as inevitable, systems of thought simply as groups of similar ideas suggesting meaning and analyticism as one major aspect of the entire area of study. It might be observed that regardless of the leadership of certain noted and original thinkers in general philosophy and in educational theory, the typical college professor of such material has little adjustment to make to conform to the newer climate of thought. Since he changes at a much slower pace, he is approaching that point to which the trailblazers are regressing. He may be at the crossroads already and waiting for his leaders.

Further justification for the appearance of this volume is obvious, especially to teachers and beginning students in the field. It treats not four or five, but all the major educational theories of the Western world. Although the religious theories are not named and placed under separate chapter headings, they can be identified as belonging to one or the other of the major philosophies included here. All the significant and necessary concepts in educational theory have been at least mentioned. This volume might well be a basal textbook for the qualified teacher and the exploring student.

Particular attention has been given to the organization of subject matter and selection of terminology in order to reduce confusion and misunderstanding by the student. Broad titles such as conservatism and liberalism are not used to name major theories since each has been employed in other volumes to cover several different views. Conversely, no major position has been subdivided to produce a series of simple emphases.

The newer modes of thought, analyticism and existentialism, have been awarded more extensive examination than have the other positions. This is because they are less familiar to the average student and also more interesting. But there is no attempt to champion any one particular theory, and every effort has been expended to present an unbiased view. If the reader is unable to identify the author with any of the theories discussed in the following pages, then one goal of the writer has been achieved.

Underlying every educational theory, there are identifiable assumptions, philosophical in nature, developed in the course of history, and each with some important relationships. This volume presents a simplified view of the supporting general philosophy, traces the development both of those assumptions and the related meaning in educational thought. The association of general philosophy with educational theory is indicated when it is apparent, but the connection is not forced. Of special interest in this regard will be the chapter on traditionalism, since this may be the first time its underlying assumptions have been structured as branches of general philosophy.

The book is not a biography of great thinkers, although most of the outstanding philosopher-educators are mentioned. Likewise, the author has not employed the "problems" approach, yet what is recorded here might well be utilized in the resolution of most of our educational perplexities.

There is one further point that needs expression; this has to do with the student who uses this book. Most prospective educators begin even their advanced studies with little background in general philosophy. If some areas of this volume appear somewhat less complex than they really are, this should be interpreted as an effort to aid these beginners where they need it. Further, with every theory presented there is a discussion of its application to the teacher, the student, the curricula, and to the society as a whole. In brief, it provides the neophyte with something to think about, to evaluate, to apply, and to analyze.

William H. Howick

TABLE OF CONTENTS

Page

Preface--- **vii**

Chapter

I. PHILOSOPHY AND EDUCATION------------------------------------- **1**

The Relationship of Philosophy to Education, 1; Guidelines for Dilettanti in Philosophy, 2; The Nature of Philosophy, 6; Major Divisions of Philosophy, 9; Nature of Educational Philosophy, 12.

II. TRADITIONALISM, THE DEMAND FOR DISCIPLINE--------------- **17**

First Phase—Religious Traditionalism, 17; Second Phase—Secular Traditionalism, 22; Current Status of Traditionalism, 25; Evaluation and Criticism, 26.

III. PROGRESSIVISM, THE PROOF FROM PRAGMATISM------------- **29**

The Development of Progressivism, 29; Pragmatism, the Philosophical Basis of Progressivism, 33; Progressivism in Education, 38; Evaluation and Criticism, 40.

IV. ESSENTIALISM, THE IDEAL ELEMENTS------------------------------ **45**

Idealism as a Basic Philosophy, 45; Essentialism, the Educational Theory, 49; Evaluation and Criticism, 53.

Chapter *Page*

V. CLASSICAL REALISM, THE PERMANENCY OF THE PERENNIAL   55

The Historical and Philosophical Basis, 55; Classical Realism as a School of Educational Philosophy, 61; Evaluation and Criticism, 66.

VI. RECONSTRUCTIONISM, THE SOCIOLOGICAL SOLUTION   69

Historical Background, 69; Philosophical Foundations of Social Reconstructionism, 71; Educational Theory and Practice, 73; Evaluation and Criticism, 76.

VII. ANALYTIC PHILOSOPHY, THE POSITIVE POSITION   79

The Historical Development of Analyticism, 79; Present Position, 87; Education and Analyticism, 91; Evaluation and Criticism, 94.

VIII. EXISTENTIALISM, THE ENCOUNTER WITH SUBJECTIVITY   97

Historical Development, 97; Philosophical Position, 103; Existentialism's Effects on Education, 111; Evaluation and Criticism, 116.

Index   119

Chapter I

PHILOSOPHY AND EDUCATION

A. THE RELATIONSHIP OF PHILOSOPHY
TO EDUCATION

Philosophy and education are two closely related academic areas. It is probable that these disciplines have as much in common as any other two major fields of study. A number of the great Greek thinkers in ancient times, particularly Plato and Aristotle, concerned themselves both with philosophical questions in general and with the particulars of education. This inclination to view the two fields as one can be seen throughout history and is evidenced in the works of such philosopher-educators as John Locke, Immanuel Kant, Johann Herbart, and the American, John Dewey, to name but a few.

But origin and development do not constitute the only similarity. A further point has to do with the remarkable degree to which the topics treated by philosophy and education coincide. These two academic areas are both vitally interested in man, his nature, knowledge, relationships, and his behavior. Likewise there is a shared interest in the good society, the good state, and the good life.

Both philosophy and education exhibit an irrepressible inclination to systematize content, to organize ideas into groups, and to develop methods. The demand for rational thought presented in logical sequence remains a major approach by philosophers. It is also one of the primary goals of most educators in recent centuries.

There was a time in the history of Western thought when, according to the earliest records available, general philosophy and education were contained in one and the same academic field. He who

1

studied one almost invariably studied the other. Even today, to acquire knowledge in either discipline void of the other results in a warped perspective. A recognition of the close relationship here will provide philosophers with a field for the application of their principles, and for educators a foundation and a much needed sense of direction.

B. GUIDELINES FOR DILETTANTI IN PHILOSOPHY

The close relationship between the fields of philosophy and education has already been indicated, but there is one further point which has been reserved until now. It is that there are probably no two fields which are more misunderstood and misinterpreted than these. The reasons for this situation are of note. First, every man with rare exception has his own ideas concerning education; he also has his own concepts about almost every other area commonly treated in general philosophy. This un-examined adherence or allegiance to isolated fragments of home-spun philosophy and educational theory, usually borrowed from others, is very difficult to overcome. Coupled with the foregoing is an aversion to the abstractness of the subject matter. Comprehension of the theoretical often requires the investment of long and even painful hours of contemplation. These characteristics have frightened away many would-be students in both general philosophy and in educational theory.

Perhaps we should regress one further step and identify another cause of this antipathy to abstract thinking. It seems that for too many years teachers to some degree have deprived their students of opportunities to develop the ability to relate abstract ideas. Instead they have attempted to provide meaning almost exclusively by the use of pictures and objects. The learners have little occasion to think in philosophical fashion. As they mount the ladder of education, so do their problems in dealing with pure thought. Likewise, the teachers have had increasingly less experience in organizing, presenting, and defending philosophical concepts. So, both students and their instructors, not to mention society as a whole, have suffered from the inclination of modern civilization to promote particulars over universal and abstract ideas.

An analysis of students' difficulties in handling philosophical material has resulted in the identification of a series of causal factors. The following list is intended to assist the student in the interpretation and application of philosophical data.

1. Everyone a Philosopher

Philosophizing is a universal pastime. There is no one who has not accepted some abstract concepts, and usually these notions are in a variety of areas. The most common are in religion, art, science, and education. In each case, one's ideas concerning that field constitute his philosophy. Every time one expresses an opinion or makes an evaluation he is philosophizing on that subject.

The major differences between the layman and the professional in philosophy are that the latter is inclined to develop his ideas more completely, to follow the lines of logic and consistency, and to put his ideas on paper. But even the man who states, "I have no time for philosophy," is at that moment philosophizing about philosophy. The inclination to theorize is not only universal; it is almost inevitable.

2. Every Thinker an Eclectic

It would be almost impossible to find a thinker today who adheres purely to one particular school or movement in philosophy. The "either/or" position is difficult to defend. It is necessary for purposes of study that we identify leaders in philosophy and educational theory with certain groups of ideas on the basis of the major tendencies which their writings exhibit. But in most instances the philosophy of any one person contains elements of several other theoretical positions, one of which is dominant.

This tendency to incorporate in one philosophy what has been taken from several other sources is known as eclecticism. Well-developed systems of philosophy aim toward purity, but most individual men in thought and practice tend to be eclectic. Serious problems are generated by this inclination to select concepts from different sources. Subjectivity enters and decreases consistency often leading one to contradictory and illogical positions.

3. The Schools of Thought

The natural propensity to associate thinkers on the basis of the similarity of their ideas is also seen in the grouping of the ideas themselves into systems or movements. A highly structured system is usually referred to as a school of thought as, for example, pragmatism in general philosophy and its counterpart in education, progressivism. Other newer and less structured groups of ideas are often termed movements.

During the 1960's there was a growing aversion to the study of educational theory by the "schools" approach. To some degree this objection grew out of the erroneous assumption by many students that the schools of eductional theory were like rigid blocks of solid logic, instead of trends, or winds of thought, or perhaps like so many streams supplying the flow of a great river of human discourse. A modified and synthetic approach to educational theory that views the schools only as convenient groupings which may then be treated analytically has a number of advantages. For students new to the field, the grouping of ideas provides a structure that is fairly easily understood and thus facilitates learning. Plunging directly into philosophical analysis of educational concepts is fine for the mind already trained in the manipulation of abstract relationships. But the typical teacher-prospect in the schools is rarely so prepared and needs first to synthesize the fundamentals of philosophy after which there will be something to analyze.

It should also be observed that the modified "schools" approach provides a series of assumptions, named or implied, against which we may check both our deductions and our practices. Goals, too, may be analyzed best when there is some stated measure alongside which they may be laid.

4. The Climate of Thought

Philosophy is a search for truth. But this does not mean that educational theorists will some day evolve the perfect structure and present the world with the one, true and final version. Most theory is responsive to changes in the thinking of the people, to changes in social structure, in politics, and in technology. The climate of thought is a fusion of the effects of all major events and developments, and man's theories operate within that milieu, not in a vacuum.

Each group of thinkers champions the cause which to its supporters appears to contain the greatest degree of truth. Individuals of different persuasion and from within the same camps express views somewhat at variance with those of their colleagues. But it is an error to assume that the differences are personal and that human relationships have been strained or severed. On the contrary, a strong sense of appreciation exists. The different emphases help theorists to keep their balance as they pace one another in the unending search for truth.

5. Differences Versus Similarities

The majority of writers and teachers treating the subject matter of the schools of philosophy, and, especially those dealing with educational theory, emphasize the differences between the several bodies of thought. It is an attempt to simplify, even to oversimplify, so as to give direction to the learner. But when the differences are emphasized, this is not to say that there are no similarities between the various schools of thought. Ideas and men are grouped on the basis of a high degree of agreement of ideas and a relatively smaller degree of variance.

Several principles need to be stated here. First, when there is a point of similarity between two schools of thought or between two thinkers from different schools, one should not assume that, therefore, these two positions are exactly the same. Second, it should be observed that although two schools, or thinkers, may emphasize a common point, this does not mean overall agreement in theory and/or in practice. For example, both progressivism and existentialism have much to say about the importance of the individual and his freedom, but they differ in interpretation. This brings us to a third principle, which is simply that many of the differences in theory, though significant and vital, are differences in degree of emphasis. A further directive would be to ask in each instance, whether a similarity or a difference, "How basic is this tenet to the position of the entire theory?" One difference, great or small, does not generate a new school of thought, and one similarity between two schools does not equate them. After all, the "schools" are artificial groupings for purposes of academic study and understanding.

C. THE NATURE OF PHILOSOPHY

Philosophy is an activity in which the substance is often highly abstract. It may well be one of the oldest, if not the oldest, of all the so-called disciplines. Yet, it is more than that. Philosophy is often a method for the exploration of the conceptual and the determination of truth. Further, philosophy is an attitude to be developed which is reflected in one's view of man and his universe. Philosophers like to think of their approach as the highest level of human thought. The following word picture will illustrate.

1. The Philosophical Approach

Let us say that four different men are standing in various places along the shore line of a particularly beautiful expanse of water. It is early morning and the surface of the lake, except for the occasional ripple, is placid. Trees shimmering in the morning dew line the banks, and a golden sun can be seen climbing from the distant horizon into an azure sky. The first man sees water and sun for the crops in neighboring fields and perhaps timber for housing and fish for food. His response to "What is it?" would be that he sees the possibility of satisfying the physical needs of man. This is the material level and many men never see above this mundane concern for existence. A more elevated view is demonstrated by the second man for he sees more than water, wood, and warmth. His view tends to break up the material into constituent parts, to see everything as elements and compounds, and to record their material relationships in terms of cause and effect. His view illustrates the level of what we may call the scientific. A third man exalts in the beauty which lies before him. The golden sun, the verdant bloom, and the sparkling waters may motivate him to compose a sonata, a poem, or a descriptive piece of prose. His response is that of the affective domain, and to the question, "What is it?" he answers that he is looking at the quality, harmony, pattern, and colors generously provided by nature. His approach is that of an artist; that is the emotive level.

The fourth man observes the same picturesque landscape as the other three viewers have done. But he is less concerned with supplying the physical needs of man, and he is not primarily interested in elements or atoms. Although he has much in common with the artist who enjoys the emotive and appreciative view, his approach is one further step removed. When for him we pose the question, "What is it?" and cite the answers of those who answered previously, his reply is in terms of more questions. He asks, "What is the basic stuff of the universe? What is beauty? What is man's relationship to his universe?" This is the philosophical attitude and its approach is practiced to some degree by all rational men. It might be added that water-watching tends to make most men philosophers even as it did the ancient Milesians.

2. Philosophy Defined

A common and literal interpretation of the word "philosophy" is "love of wisdom." But it is much more. Philosophy is concerned with basic considerations and underlying assumptions. Its subject matter is abstract and is not ordinarily susceptible to analyzation by scientists and mathematicians. It inquires into principles of reality, knowledge, and value and tends to group its answers into related schools and systems of thought. Philosophy is the rational approach to problems and questions in contrast to the purely materialistic, scientific, or emotive. It is a comprehensive and reasoned inquiry dealing with the foundations in thought of all human activity, especially in the fields of science, art, religion, and education. It does not provide answers as much as it questions answers.

3. Philosophical Approaches

Historically, philosophers have approached the content of their field in one of three ways. They have been speculative, prescriptive, or critical and analytical. The nature of the subject matter to a large extent has determined the degree to which one approach or another has been employed.

The ancient Greek philosophers during the cosmological period were concerned with the nature of the universe. Their studies did not grow from a base of scientific principles, since there was comparatively little concrete scientific knowledge in existence. So, they employed speculation, and until recent decades, metaphysics has remained speculative.

When the early Greek metaphysicians began to perceive that they were not able to formulate answers to questions concerning reality that would be final and satisfactory to all men, they turned from cosmology to a consideration of the nature of knowledge. Although many of the early thinkers were still speculative, the tendency now was to become prescriptive. This was especially true with the development of studies in value, including ethics and aesthetics. Many of the early philosophers employed the critical and analytical approach as can be seen in their writings. Now in a more modern day, philosophy has become less speculative, hardly prescriptive, and strongly critical. Currently, many maintain that the philosophers have discarded the good while disposing the bad, and they would like philosophy to return to utilizing all three approaches.

Philosophy is speculative when it considers the highly abstract questions dealing with the nature of reality. Here, philosophy seeks a unified view and demands order and pattern in the universe. The prescriptive approach is best seen when philosophy treats the problems of what is good and beautiful or bad and ugly. Then it sets up norms and separates the "is" from the "ought." Critical attitudes are evidenced when philosophers analyze concepts, for example "truth," "education," and "knowledge." Here the thinker is interested in clarification, interpretation, and verified meaning.

4. The Values of Philosophy

A compilation of all the benefits of philosophy would result in a list too long and tedious to hold the interest of the most highly motivated student. Presented here will be the major values only.

1. Philosophy endeavors to provide a comprehensive view of man and his universe. The physical sciences must necessarily separate the universe piece by piece, element from element, but philosophy attempts to see everything as a unified whole and in proper relationship.
2. Philosophy tends to develop the ability to deal with abstract ideas, to ask intelligent questions, and to formulate rational answers. Clarity, consistency, and objectivity result from the study of this field.
3. Philosophy gives direction, especially in religion and education. There may be no area more valuable and practical than the theoretical. This study assists in the choosing of desirable goals, means, and purposes. It offers principles for truth, not fixed answers.

D. MAJOR DIVISIONS OF PHILOSOPHY

Classical schools of philosophy have divided the content of philosophical studies into three branches. These divisions can be seen in almost every presentation made of the tenets of idealism and realism. Even the more modern school of American pragmatism fits into the same scheme. More recently, some interpreters of existentialism have presented the principles of that movement using this same organization which follows here. The three major divisions are metaphysics, logic or epistemology, and axiology.

1. Metaphysics

Metaphysics asks the question, "What is reality?" "Physics" refers to the physical world or the cosmos, while the prefix "meta" has come to mean that which transcends nature and has value apart from the material universe. Metaphysics, thus, is concerned with abstract questions which cannot be treated by the purely scientific approaches of observation and experimentation. The content of the study includes such topics as universals versus particulars, time and space, the nature of things, of mind, of change, and motion, and the relationship of concepts to each other. The term ontology, once a subdivision in the study of philosophy which dealt with being, is now generally employed synonymously with metaphysics.

Aristotle called his writings on this subject, first philosophy. The term, metaphysics, was not introduced until the first century B.C., probably by Andronicus of Rhodes. Aristotle's metaphysics focuses on the universe which he explains is comprised of a great number of finite things and which can be grouped in categories or classes. Things are known by the characteristics they exhibit and we identify and classify in keeping with the experiences we have with them. There is movement from potentiality to actuality, brought about by a changeless, immaterial, prime mover, or unmoved mover.

Metaphysics historically has attempted to understand the universe by a priori investigation. Its method has been abstract and concerned with principles in contrast to the method of the physical sciences which deals with material evidence as known by the senses. But there has been considerable variation among philosophers both as to the questions to be included in the study as well as in the answers proposed. Pre-Socratic philosophers sought for a basic "stuff" that would serve as the key for unlocking the mysteries of the universe. They suggested water, air, earth, fire, numbers, atoms, and other aspects as essences. Thomas Aquinas (1225-1274) proposed a religious metaphysics based on an interpretation of Aristotle. René Descartes (1596-1650) wrote at length about matter and mind and tended to make metaphysics more scientific and mathematical. John Locke (1632-1704), a follower of Descartes, dealt with substance and essence, while Immanuel Kant (1724-1804) questioned whether metaphysics could be treated as an exact science. Kant turned to a study of reason by the use of reason.

Metaphysics as a fruitful field of study has been under increasing attack since the days of Georg Friedrich Hegel (1770-1831). The extreme idealism of Hegel's metaphysics contributed to the rise of existentialism and analyticism, both of which until recently had little regard for metaphysical bases. Now, once again, philosophy is returning to the "silent metaphysics" which has always been present and ever served as a foundation for both scientific and the philosophical structures even though criticized and disregarded.

2. *Logic-Epistemology*

To reduce this branch of philosophy to one question, would be to ask "What is truth?" The inability of ancient thinkers to provide final and satisfactory answers to their metaphysical questions precipitated the move toward a consideration of the origin, nature, structure, and extent of human knowing. This study is also concerned with the methods to be employed in determining truth and the validity of claims to knowledge. In contrast to psychology which explains why men believe certain propositions, epistemology is concerned with the ground or basis for truth presented.

Logic, as a related field, treats inferences and proof; it studies syntax and semantics. Aristotle, founder of studies in ancient logic, made extensive use of the syllogism with its major premise, minor premise, and valid or invalid inference. Some thinkers have maintained that man cannot know real truth about anything, as in the case of the Skeptics in the fifth century B. C. Others have held that knowledge is based on a realm of forms and the truth to which men hold are mere copies of these unchanging universals. In a more modern day, some philosophers have promoted the belief that truth is personal and every man must develop his own.

Historically, the study of logic has included many topics which were later regarded as epistemological. Eventually, logicians began to limit their studies to the science of principles governing valid reasoning, while epistemology dealt with the nature of truth. But the distinction between the two is not a major concern here. It is important however, to note that logic may be either formal, of which Aristotle's syllogism is an example, or material. The latter involves certain methodologies for finding truth as authoritarianism, mysticism or revelation, experimentalism or empiricism, rationalism, pragmatism, and may even include skepticism. The divisions of deduction and induction describe contrasting types of logic employed in the pursuit and verification of truth.

3. *Axiology*

The question here might well be, "What is value?" Axiology first appeared as a separate study with Plato where it was related to his metaphysics involving ideas and particulars in separate realms. Aristotle further developed the field, and, by the time of Aquinas, some

of its questions had become of major concern to Christian philosophers. By the nineteenth century, axiology had spread so that it involved not only religion, but psychology, the humanities, and the
social sciences, especially education. Axiology tends to categorize
values in two broad areas—namely, aesthetic and ethical—which ask the
questions, "What is beauty?" and "What is good?" respectively. It is
primarily concerned with the "oughtness," not the "isness" of a situation.

The topics treated by this branch of philosophy are several. Most
axiologists begin with discussions on the nature of value, and their
answers are widely divergent. Some have held that valuation is based
on desire or pleasure while others at the opposite end of the spectrum
insist that valuing is purely pragmatic. The relationship of axiology
to the various branches of philosophy, especially to metaphysical concepts, has been extensively treated; likewise the problem of criteria or
standards for valuing. One further question has to do with types of
value. An intrinsic one has innate worth and is thus valued for its
own sake, such as the good, the beautiful, or the holy. On the other
hand, there are extrinsic or instrumental values which are means or
tools to human betterment. John Dewey is remembered as one who
vigorously objected to such distinctions as intrinsic and extrinsic and
ends versus means.

E. NATURE OF EDUCATIONAL PHILOSOPHY

That all questions, when investigated and traced to their origins,
become philosophical in nature, is a postulate proposed in this volume. History may deal with the development of ideas, while sociology
may describe the effects of their application. And every other field of
study, likewise, has its particular and overlapping responsibility. Yet,
the final questions in every area are philosophical. Education is certainly no exception to this principle.

When the key considerations in any field of study are traced back
and restated in their ultimate form, this does not necessarily mean
that one eventually arrives at some fixed system of thought which
must be accepted *in toto*. The philosopher's penchant for organization
and design must not again lead us to commit that error. This does

not mean, though, that every fundamental question is completely different from every other. Grouping is still possible and desirable, if not necessary. Educational philosophy like general philosophy has chosen to place most of its fundamental questions in three untied packages called branches, to wit, metaphysics, logic-epistemology, and axiology.

1. Metaphysics in Education

Metaphysics investigates principles of reality which transcend the various fields of science, physical and behavioral. It concerns itself with ultimate questions or "first philosophy." Although exceedingly abstract, metaphysical questions often support educational inquiries. The teacher who states, "I educate for reality," has told us nothing until he also answers the question, "What is reality?" Reality might be the material world of particulars known by the senses, contemporary personal and social considerations, or it may refer to a body of universal truths in some realm entirely non-material and non-human, for example, the realities of religion. Classes in the sciences, literature, and history appear to have the most direct and frequent contacts with metaphysical questions. The teacher who has not clearly and thoroughly considered and decided what reality is for him will not be qualified to guide students' questions when they are relevant to metaphysics. Since such ontological considerations are basic to statements of goals and purposes in education, failure or weakness here could undermine an entire program of learning.

2. Logic-Epistemology in Education

Specifically, epistemology concerns itself with the nature of truth, while logic deals with the principles of valid reasoning. The approach of both is in terms of knowledge, in which case it is extremely difficult to see how any educator could function intelligently without an understanding of this branch of philosophy. The teacher who has developed a working knowledge of logic and epistemology can differentiate between truth and opinion. He knows that all which is called education is not necessarily knowledge, that truth is obtainable only when the subjective aspects are restrained, and that good teaching requires careful organization of the subject matter so as to indicate proper sequence, cause and effect, and relative importance. The truly professional teacher recognizes flaws and fallacies in the course of classroom discussion. He is quick to distinguish deductive from inductive reasoning, and formal logic employing the syllogism from material logic. The logician is aware that no one method may be employed in every situation, and that the choice is determined mainly by the nature of the subject matter under investigation. One does not study eternal verities with an atom smasher or analyze atoms theologically. The teacher trained in logic also knows that similes, metaphors, and examples are not evidences or proofs of truth but simply windows through which what is stated may be seen more clearly.

3. *Axiology in Education*

Axiology is a study of values and may be separated into aesthetics and ethics with the latter field further divided into personal or social ethics. The question common to all divisions of axiology is, "What is good?" Neither axiologists nor educators are primarily interested in erecting value systems but rather with the ground upon which judgments of good, bad, or ugly rest. Valuation is not exercised in a vacuum. Rather, each valuative expression is based on some fundamental principles which ideally have received adequate consideration prior to their acceptance.

A practitioner in the field of education might conceivably disregard the relationship of metaphysics to education. It would be considerably more difficult to operate a learning program without giving some thought to the importance of logic and epistemology. But axiological questions are constantly faced by the educator. Teachers and students alike evaluate the capabilities and conduct of each other concurrent with the evolvement of judgments of the subject matter, methods, and textbooks. Concrete examples of such appraisal can be seen in the labels of good or bad attached to literary works, interpretations of history, the importance of one study as compared to another, to name but a few. Meanwhile, the supporting society evaluates the total educational system including programs, personnel, benefits and goals. A teacher who has not personally identified those principles which lead toward and support the good state, the good society, and the good life is hardly qualified to recognize the good school and the good student.

FURTHER READING

Baldwin, James Mark (ed.). *Dictionary of Philosophy and Psychology*, Vols. I, II, and III. New York: The Macmillan Company, 1928.

Brameld, Theodore. *Philosophies of Education in Cultural Perspective*. New York: The Dryden Press, Inc., 1955.

Edwards, Paul (ed. in chief). *The Encyclopedia of Philosophy*, Vols. I-VIII. New York: The Macmillan Company and the Free Press, 1967.

Ennis, Robert H. "Can Philosophy of Education Be Relevant?" *Educational Theory*, Vol. 20, Number 4 (Fall, 1970), pp. 337-344.

Jones, W. T. *A History of Western Philosophy*. New York: Harcourt, Brace and Company, 1952.

Lucas, Christopher J. "Some Second Thoughts About Metaphysics in Educational Theory," *Educational Theory*. Vol. 20, No. 2 (Spring, 1970), pp. 129-142.

Peters, Francis E. *Greek Philosophical Terms*. New York: New York University Press, 1967.

Runes, Dagobert D. (ed.). *Dictionary of Philosophy*. New York: Philosophical Library, Inc., 1942.

Stoops, John A. *Philosophy and Education in Western Civilization*. Danville, Illinois: The Interstate Printers & Publishers, Inc., 1971.

Chapter II

TRADITIONALISM,

The Demand for Discipline

The educational philosophy which has characterized American education for more years than any other is that of traditionalism. However, this school of thought has not always been known by that term. The reference, formalism, appeared just prior to the turn of the twentieth century and was employed mainly during that transitional period in American history when the society moved from the predominantly religious motif to a concern for the secular aspects of life. Since World War II the title, intellectual discipline, has been in common use. The name traditionalism has been utilized here because it is the most comprehensive, referring both to the historic backgrounds and the contemporary emphasis of its modern supporters.

A. FIRST PHASE—RELIGIOUS TRADITIONALISM
(1630-1875)

The Historical Background

The Pilgrims who came to the shores of the New World in the early 1600's were known as Separatists. It is true, of course, that they had separated themselves from the Church of England as far as membership was concerned. Yet they had not separated themselves from the theology and practices of the religion of their time. On the contrary, they had brought their beliefs with them and imposed these ideas on many of the inhabitants of the New World. This imported version of faith and practice, somewhat modified to serve particular purposes, has become known as Puritanism.

Puritan Religion and Philosophy

1. Social Philosophy

Colonial America adopted a social philosophy that was religion-centered. Consistent with that theme, early Puritans related every development to religion and almost every minor act to the presumed will of God. In such a setting the church necessarily became the basic social institution and its ministers authorities of power and prestige. Furthermore, since the majority of these people were Calvinistic in doctrine, the entire social hierarchy developed the concept that one's position in life as well as in eternity was predetermined. This climate of thought demanded that the citizens accept the social hierarchy as divinely ordained and then quietly obey their religious superiors. An old English hymn writer expressed the same idea:

> The rich man in his castle,
> The poor man at his gate
> God made them high and lowly
> And ordered their estate.

Thus, there was determinism in the present and preparatory existence, and predestination with regard to the hereafter.

2. Metaphysical Position

The fundamental concept in Puritan thought was the doctrine of divinity. God was omnipotent, omniscient and omnipresent. As the opposite of evil, He hated sin and was often angry at evildoers. A good example of the religious teachings of the period is found in the famous sermon, "Sinners in the Hands of an Angry God," by one of America's great theologians and philosophers, Jonathan Edwards (1703-1758).

This sovereign power was also the antithesis of matter. He was conceptual, universal and thus eternal. God could not be material for that would make for transiency. He was not limited by time and space for that would make for temporalness. Although God created the world, He was not to be regarded as part of it. Rather, He was spiritual, perfect, and holy while matter was essentially evil.

Matter was evil, but not only because it was the opposite of spirit. The desires of men for material possessions often enticed them to build for the temporal rather than the eternal life. And a paramount evidence of the inherent evil of matter was the human body. Paradoxically, God's crowning creation, namely man, was housed in a temple that had evil appetites and unholy desires which had to be suppressed. Furthermore, the human body forced man to live in a wicked world, imprisoning his spirit that feign would fly away to rejoin its Creator in a blissful eternity.

3. *Epistemological Position*

To the Puritan mind, God was not only true reality; He was also real truth. Knowledge had to begin and end with divinity. All other truth was subordinate to religious dogma, and if any contradiction existed, the interpretation of the Christian Bible by the ministry prevailed.

The mind of carnal man, however, was in no condition to fully comprehend real truth. Because Adam in the Garden of Eden had willfully transgressed the known will of God, sin had entered the human race. Thereafter all the offspring of mankind were born depraved in mind and spirit. The warped mind thought evil continually and needed to be disciplined and straightened. Even the newborn were baptized to "seal" them from the curse of Adam until they reached the "age of accountability," at which time they would, hopefully, follow the footsteps of their Biblical namesakes.

4. *Axiological Position*

Ethically, man was by nature an evil being. Thus, there was nothing good about the newborn child. He had been "born in sin and shapen in iniquity" and could do none other than choose the wrong and that continually. Parents were expected to force the child to accept the religious taboos and conform to the social pattern of the day in order to save the child from himself and final damnation.

Aesthetics was not an area of study that enjoyed much favor under Puritanism. Even the beauties of the great outdoors seemed to hold little attraction for the minds of these people. Their existence here was only preparatory, and happiness was to be expected only after they had overcome that evil spirit, the Devil, and arrived safely inside Heaven's jasper walls. The concern for life after death overshadowed any interest in the betterment of life after birth. In aesthetics, as elsewhere, the notion persisted that whatever was human and natural was bad. Delight itself was a natural response and was therefore evil. The fine arts, especially music and painting, were frowned upon. Literary appreciation was limited to the Bible, the Psalter, and the few other books which appeared later in the period.

Consequent Educational Practices

1. The Purposes of Education

"As the society, so is the school" was probably never more true than it was among the early Puritans. A religion-centered society demanded an educational program that was in keeping with the prevailing theological position. If human nature was evil, then the school should aid in the bringing of youthful spirits into subjection and their souls to eternal salvation.

Furthermore, education should reinforce the existing social and religious patterns of the community. Since the society was organized and operated by adults, who, because of years of effort, had presumably made considerable progress from depravity toward holiness, these leaders obviously knew best. The school's task, then, was to add strength to that position by the use of rigid discipline, through its lockstep curriculum, and by a constant emphasis on religion. On the books in the Connecticut Colony were rules which held: "No one shall travel, cook victuals, make beds, sweep house, cut hair or shave on the Sabbath Day." And, also, "Every male shall have his hair cut around according to a cap." It is fairly obvious that the clergy and adults in general used religion to their own advantage, rather than the reverse, as it was intended. Perhaps these people who saw God only as vindictive and demanding were reflecting their own warped personalities. That the Puritan ethic was more enshrined than observed is evidence of the hypocrisy which arises from extreme regimentation.

2. The Importance of Discipline

The doctrine of natural depravity permeates Puritan education. The great Saint Augustine taught this doctrine emphasizing the need for discipline and thus set the pattern for most schools with religious purposes. If children are naturally bad, then whatever activities are natural for them would be evil. Laughter, dancing, and play are evil because they spring from the human and natural desires of children and were to be tolerated to a limited degree. Under no circumstances should these and related activities be permitted in church or in school. On the other hand, teachers were to control their charges by regimentation and severe discipline including the use of the rod. One early schoolmaster is reported to have said, "A boy has a back. If you beat it, he understands."

The Puritan schoolroom was, thus, not a very cheerful environment. There were no chalkboards or bulletin boards, pictures or decorations of any kind. Most of these early schools did not even have the benefit of a tuning fork, since such instruments had been known to lead the young and depraved down the path to eternal perdition. The fact that so many of the learners responded with negative attitudes towards all schooling and teachers and protested by behaving badly only caused their elders to be more convinced of the doctrine of innate depravity.

3. The Methods Employed

Children in the early Puritan schools were subjected to the traditional procedure of assignment, memorization, and recitation. The teacher needed to know very little since there was practically no instruction demanded of him. In the main, he simply assigned the material which was to be memorized, and then, often with his own copy in hand, he listened to the children recite their lessons. There was some teaching by question and answer but little discussion and hardly any attention paid to reflection and meaning. It might be added that the almost exclusive use of the oral method was probably due to the unavailability and the high cost of paper. The apparent belief in innate ideas, a doctrine denied by John Locke, was also a factor and gave rise to the traditional methods of teaching reading and the emphasis on spelling in the Colonial schoolrooms in which cases meaningfulness was simply assumed.

4. The Curriculum

The first "R" was religion, and this subject constituted the beginning and goal of Puritan traditionalism in education. Using the hornbook or the battledore, children were taught their "letters" so as to be able to read the Bible. In this manner they also learned numerals, the Lord's Prayer, the catechism, and the Psalter. When the *New England Primer* appeared about 1690, it was added to the curriculum of the school. Its content was primarily religious and began with:

> In Adam's fall
> We sinned all.

There were, however, some lines in the *New England Primer* that at least indicated the beginnings of a secular type of traditionalism. The coming of various spelling books from 1650 and including the famous one by Noah Webster, *The American Spelling Book*, further developed this trend in the course of history.

B. SECOND PHASE—SECULAR TRADITIONALISM (1875 TO THE PRESENT)

1. The Transition to a Secular Society

During the latter part of the Colonial Period, American society moved from the predominantly religious-centered community to a more secular mode. The influences which precipitated this change were numerous and interrelated. The physical sciences, for example, had extended their investigations to the point where it appeared that traditional religious concepts would be seriously undermined. Darwin's theory of evolution, in particular, challenged the faith of orthodox Christians. Yet with the assistance of modern science, man's temporal existence progressed more rapidly than ever from the harsh and menial to one of enjoyment and leisure. In turn, the freedom from the relentless demands of making a living provided man with an opportunity for reflection on his world and on life in general. This situation was further enhanced by that period of comparative peace which followed the last armed conflict of the nineteenth century, the Spanish American War in 1898, and the concern for social justice under President Theodore Roosevelt during the first decade of the twentieth century .

In addition to the scientific and socio-political forces, and most important of all, was the changing philosophical climate during this period. The average American had achieved a higher level of education and was better informed than most of his preceding countrymen. He was also more curious, enjoyed more freedom, and was less willing to accept and submit to the so-called superiors, including church dignitaries. He behaved differently because he thought differently. The better-educated clergymen themselves were beginning to speak of a God much less angry at sinful man and more eager to save him than man was to save himself. Such literary figures as Ralph Waldo Emerson and Henry David Thoreau, of the mid-nineteenth century, contributed a more acceptable approach to the idea of God. The new concept emphasized divine love in place of divine wrath.

Meanwhile the principles of utilitarianism followed by those of American pragmatism were permeating the life and thoughts of Western man. The emphasis had shifted from "otherworldliness" to "this worldliness." Hereafter man was to view his life, not only as a period of preparation for the hereafter, but as a value in itself. Man was now to enjoy life and improve his situation.

2. Secular Traditionalism

One of the problems of our modern and changing world is that all segments of a given society do not change at the same time or at the same rate. American education is a prime example of this incongruity. It took more time, and the movement is still in progress, for the typical American public school to move from a religion-centered ethical discipline to a subject-centered intellectual discipline. Even then, the transition from the first phase to the second and present did not alter all aspects of traditional education. Many principles and practices remained unchanged and others simply were modified to suit a more modern society.

The hierarchy of control which characterized Colonial education can be seen in many school systems and individual institutions of learning today. Likewise, one may visit schools and colleges whose programs of instruction are logically structured according to the adult mind. Such institutions usually insist that every student's work be evaluated by fixed, unchanging standards. The resulting general atmosphere is thought by some to be quite academic but is regarded by the critics as oppressive and disciplinary.

With the major exception of the religious emphasis, the secular type of traditional school maintains a curriculum which has much in common with that followed by the Colonial schools. One authority, Clifton Fadiman, speaks of the generative power of certain subjects and of others which are simply self-terminating.[1] These generative subjects which constitute the curriculum of a school dedicated to intellectual discipline have been named by Dr. Arthur Bestor as one's mother tongue, foreign language, history, mathematics, and the sciences.[2] Present day supporters of traditionalism object to much of what constitutes the program of the modern school. They oppose the social, psychological, recreational, and even the vocational concerns of American public education.

The teacher-centered classroom of modern traditionalism continues to place great emphasis on drill and memorization. No longer can these educators defend such methods on the basis that paper is in short supply. So they have turned to emphasizing the transmission of

1. Clifton Fadiman, in *The Case for Basic Education*, edited by James D. Koerner (Boston: Little, Brown and Company, 1959), pp. 5-6.
2. Arthur Bestor, in *Philosophies of Education*, edited by Philip H. Phenix (New York: John Wiley and Sons, Inc., 1965), p. 38.

the content of traditionally-accepted fields of study, the intellectual benefits of a well-furnished mind, and the importance of reason in human life. School and society are still separated and there is little relationship between what transpires in the classroom and life on the outside, although a transfer of training is necessarily assumed to take place. If "faculty psychology" is not part of the theory it is at least part of the practice. Modern traditionalism, however emancipated from Puritan religion, is still tied to the bookish discipline of the past.

C. CURRENT STATUS OF TRADITIONALISM

In the 1950's, two vigorous supporters of intellectual discipline began their attacks on the American public school system. One was Dr. Arthur Bestor, now of the University of California, and a noted historian. Dr. Bestor's evaluation of American education is well expressed by the title of his best-known book, namely, *Educational Wastelands, or The Retreat from Learning in Our Schools.*[3] He attacks the proliferation of courses, the current emphasis on social adjustment, the importance given to athletics, and the educational bureaucracy, among other things. Admiral G. Hyman Rickover of the United States Navy also expresses similar views in his book, *Education and Freedom.*[4]

Intellectual discipline is not a school in the sense of having affected an organization. However, in the absence of such a group, some supporters have become affiliated with the Council for Basic Education, Washington, D. C. In fact, Dr. Bestor, and also Clifton Fadiman, both of whom were quoted earlier in the chapter, have served as members of the Board of Directors of that organization. This is not to say, however, that the Council for Basic Education functions to support any particular school of educational thought even though there is a considerable degree of similarity between the stand taken by some members of the Council and the educational concepts discussed here. The emphasis on academic excellence by the Council for Basic Education has served to counteract some of the anti-intellectualism in American schools and has the approval of many leading educators.

---

3. Urbana: University of Illinois Press, 1953.
4. New York: E. P. Dutton and Co., Inc., 1959.

D. EVALUATION AND CRITICISM

Most of the criticism of traditionalism has come from secular, as opposed to religious, forces in the American community. The students themselves had objected for years, but that was before young collegians learned the importance of organization and mass protest. As a result, it fell to the progressive educators and other presumably enlightened citizens to make formal presentation of their dissent. Following is a digest of the common criticisms:

1. The basis for the theory of traditionalism is open to question. Its support comes from tradition, intuition, authoritarianism, and certain intellectual dispositions whose so-called truths cannot be verified. Historically, and even currently, there is an obvious lack of scientific evidence in support of the practices of traditionalism, say the critics.

2. Traditionalism seeks to transmit the content of certain subject areas by requiring memorization and agreement with certain fixed conclusions instead of educating learners in the method of intelligence. Its subject matter content and organization are concerned with the past instead of the present, and emphasizes the teacher in place of the student.

3. There is misunderstanding as to the real nature of the child. Traditionalism does not set the child free to learn and interact. The result is passivity and conformity.

4. The lack of a close relationship between the learning and the living of the children is a key point. John Dewey, especially, criticized any educational program which did not operate according to accepted democratic principles.

FURTHER READING

Bayles, Ernest E. and Bruce L. Hood. *Growth of American Educational Thought and Practice.* New York: Harper and Row, Publishers, 1966.
Bestor, Arthur. *Educational Wastelands.* Urbana: University of Illinois Press, 1953.
Bestor, Arthur. *The Restoration of Learning.* New York: Alfred A. Knopf Publisher, 1955.

Dupuis, Adrian M. *Philosophy of Education in Historical Perspective*. Chicago: Rand McNally and Company, 1966.

Edwards, Newton and Herman G. Richey. *The School in the American Social Order* (2nd ed.). Boston: Houghton Mifflin Company, 1963.

French, William. *America's Educational Tradition*. Boston: D. C. Heath and Company, 1964.

Koerner, James D. *The Case for Basic Education*. Boston: Little, Brown and Company, 1959.

Phenix, Phillip H. (ed.). *Philosophies of Education*. New York: John Wiley and Sons, Inc. 1965.

Rickover, H. G. *American Education, A National Failure*. New York: E. P. Dutton and Co., Inc., 1963.

Rickover, H. G. *Education and Freedom*. New York: E. P. Dutton and Co., Inc., 1959.

"Education as Intellectual Discipline," a film. New Film Service, Indiana University, Bloomington, Indiana.

Chapter III

PROGRESSIVISM,

The Proof from Pragmatism

Progressivism is primarily an American contribution to educational philosophy. It has been the most criticized and probably the least understood of all the major positions. This last has been due in part to the tendency of its proponents to change emphasis from time to time. Some advocates of the concepts subsumed under this title have preferred the name, experientialism, which directs one's attention to the primacy of experience in the process of learning. But progressivism is also allied with the modern and scientific concern for experimentation. Thus, the term, experimentalism, has often been heard. Consistent with the above, yet promoting the notion that all things are means, or at least, only ends-in-view, is the label, instrumentalism, coined by John Dewey himself. Occasionally one hears the words progressivism and pragmatism used interchangeably, which is hardly correct. Pragmatism refers to a school of thought in general philosophy, while progressivism is an expression of those concepts in the field of education. The relationship of pragmatism to progressivism is the strongest and most intimate one existing between any school of general philosophy and a differently-named theory of education.

A. THE DEVELOPMENT OF PROGRESSIVISM

1. Early Contributors

The most widely known tenets of this school of educational

0372618

thought have been that the child is the center of the learning process; the teacher should be permissive and offer guidance; and the subject matter must be related to contemporary living. That these principles were not original with early American progressives can be seen from a study of the early contributors, sometimes called pre-progressives.

a. *Quintilian (A.D. 35-95?)*

The great Roman teacher despised ancient Greek philosophy and taught that education should be practical, that is, related to contemporary life. Quintilian, furthermore, objected to the then common practice of treating children harshly, and, in contrast, advocated consideration of the learner as a person with certain rights who differed from every other person. In regard to the instructor's place, Quintilian wrote, "The eloquent teacher must be wise and ready to adapt himself to the capacity of the learner, as one who walks takes a young child by the hand to help him keep up."[1] Little heed was given to the pedagogical ideas of the great Roman school master until after his writings were rediscovered in 1410 in the monastery of St. Gall. Even then, popular interest in his works had to await the synthesis of American progressivism.

b. *Jean Jacques Rousseau*

There were many contributors to educational theory who lived and wrote during the long period of time separating Quintilian and Rousseau. A number of these thinkers expressed educational ideas that are clearly progressive in principle. This present volume, of course, can mention only the most prominent, which includes the great French philosopher, Rousseau.

The best known writing by Rousseau is probably his *Émile*, a name which implies freedom to be one's self, to be creative and spontaneous. Underlying Rousseau's demand for freedom was his belief that all children were born good. The blame for evil deeds must be attributed to a corrupt society, not innate depravity. Further, if a

---

1. Charles E. Little, *Quintilian, the Schoolmaster*, Vol. I (Nashville, Tennessee: The Peabody Press, 1951).

child is naturally good, he should not be punished by those adults over him. Rather, let nature punish him in her own way and in her own time, Rousseau held. And so, naturalism as a theory of child development and education was born.

c. Johann Heinrich Pestalozzi (1746-1827)

The great Swiss educator is credited with exerting more influence on American education than any other European thinker in history. He expressed his principles of learning in writings entitled *Leonard and Gertrude* (1782) and a sequel, *How Gertrude Teaches Her Children* (1802). To Pestalozzi, education was to fit one for life by training the hand, head, and heart in that order. He believed that effective instruction should employ concrete objects as a means to understanding, that children learn best when their studies are supported by real experiences, and that the teacher's main task is to motivate through love and affection.

2. Progressivism as a Movement in the United States

a. Pestalozzianism was formally introduced to the United States about 1809 by Joseph Neef, a co-worker of Pestalozzi at Burgdorf, Switzerland. Neef taught in Philadelphia and in Louisville, and eventually became part of the socialistic community of scientists at New Harmony, Indiana.

b. Another avenue by which Pestalozzianism reached the New World was through the influence of Horace Mann. In 1844, following his return from a six-month European trip, Mann wrote his Seventh Annual Report as chief state school officer in Massachusetts. This report was openly enthusiastic of the Pestalozzian approach to learning, and it incurred the displeasure of the Boston schoolmasters. Mann, however, continued to promote the "new learning" until he resigned his position to become a member of the United States House of Representatives.

c. Francis Wayland Parker was a noted American educator during the second half of the nineteenth century. He had distinguished himself as superintendent of schools in Quincy, Massachusetts,

and as principal of Cook County Normal School. His commitment to
Froebelian principles of education did much to promote concepts such
as "creative self-expression," and play as a means of learning. As early
as the 1870's Parker was called the "father of progressive education."
He represented a significant company of American educators who by
1900 were openly expressing their objections to the extremes of traditionalism with its passive learning and emphasis on memorization
and discipline.

d. John Dewey, meanwhile, was at the University of Chicago
and occupied with developing a philosophic basis to support the
new ideas in education. The nature of this new philosophy, namely
pragmatism, required that it be applied to some area of human activity. Dewey fortunately chose the field of education and subsequently
established in 1896 a laboratory school in connection with the University of Chicago. He declared at the time that he wanted to give children an opportunity to learn in a desirable environment and the faculty a chance to experiment with the new ideas in education. Dewey
found it necessary to leave the University of Chicago in 1909, but he
continued his work with philosophy and education at Columbia University, which resulted in the publication of his first important volume,
Democracy and Education.[2] Meanwhile, the leadership of Dewey's
laboratory school in Chicago passed into the hands of Charles H.
Judd, who favored a middle-of-the-road position.

e. The Progressive Education Association was eventually
founded in 1918 with Charles William Eliot of Harvard University as
honorary president. The periodical, *Progressive Education,* made its
appearance in 1924 and helped to spread the new approach to learning involving freedom for the child, learning through activity, and also
insisted that the teacher must never be obtrusive. Private schools at
first seemed more willing to accept the principles of progressivism,
but the public institutions could not help but undergo alteration as
well. Progressivism eventually influenced all segments of American
education, and its effects are very obvious in the classrooms today.

During the great economic depression of 1929-1939, progressivism

2. New York: The Macmillan Company, 1916.

altered its course to some degree. The threat to the country during that decade seemed to make it desirable to move from an emphasis on individual freedom to democratic cooperation. The earlier failure of some progressivists to consider social needs, as well as personal ones, rose as a criticism. A general feeling developed that a diluted educational program was to some degree responsible for the plight of society. The return to a more conservative position was led by William Chandler Bagley and the essentialists. As opposition arose to the presumed extremes and failures of progressivism, the movement lost many of its supporters. The organization changed its name in 1944 to the American Education Fellowship, then reverted to the previous title. When John Dewey died in 1952, the end seemed to many people to be in sight. By then, the Progressive Education Association had reached a point where there were too few dues-paying members to continue publication of a periodical or to function as an organization. Final disbandment occurred in 1955. The requiem was sung with the publication in 1958 of a brief article which appeared in most major newspapers of the country. Education Editor, Paul Woodring, of the *New York Times* declared that the "Progressive Cult Is Dead."[3]

However, progressivism as an educational philosophy was far from dead. Looking back, it is obvious that it was a case of arrested development.[4] Progressivism as a practical philosophy of education may have been somewhat dormant for a time, but it has never died. In fact, since the early 1960's it has been gaining ground and winning new acceptance.

B. PRAGMATISM, THE PHILOSOPHICAL BASIS OF PROGRESSIVISM

1. *Historical Development*

a. Concepts that are essentially pragmatic can be found in the writings of many of the great philosophers. Most outstanding in this connection are the works of Francis Bacon (1561-1626) and John

---

3. *Nashville Tennessean*, November 16, 1958.
4. Henry C. Johnson, Jr., "Progressive Education: A Case of Arrested Development?" *Educational Theory*, Vol. XV, No. 3, July, 1965.

Locke (1632-1704), both Englishmen. Some contributors were American and included such well-known thinkers as Benjamin Franklin, Thomas Paine, and Thomas Jefferson.

b. In addition to the influence of the aforementioned pre-pragmatists there were social and cultural developments which helped to prepare the way for a new philosophy. First, man's attitude toward life had changed. Partly because of the Industrial Revolution and the rise of experimental science, men began to look upon the temporal existence as a value in itself and one that could be altered and improved. As a consequence there was less respect for tradition, for any philosophy or religion that would support the *status quo,* and for authority in general. Here was another distinguishable move in the relentless march of man toward personal freedom. Coupled with all of this was the rise of democracy, both as a form of government and as a way of life, which in turn provided an atmosphere of freedom for thought and action. Without the nurture of American democracy, pragmatism would have been much longer in developing.

c. Pragmatism is a distinctly American contribution to the field of general philosophy. Its first formulator was Charles Sanders Peirce (1839-1914), once a student at Harvard University and later a part-time lecturer at Johns Hopkins University. His training in not only philosophy but in mathematics and chemistry provided the kind of orientation necessary to the development of the new field of thought. Peirce was probably the first to use the word "pragmatism," and later "pragmaticism," which he coined from the Greek term "pragma," interpreted as deed or action. His beginning point is simply that words have meaning when related to experience. If an idea cannot be utilized in a practical situation, then that idea has no meaning. An idea does, not just is. Thus, any idea one has must be in terms of its "sensible effects," to use Peirce's own language.

Although Peirce's pragmatism begins with thought and requires deeds and consequences, positioned between these two are beliefs, which give direction. Beliefs, however, need to be determined, and the only realistic method is that employed by the sciences. The method of science deals with real things, proven characteristics, and is independent of opinions. This approach to truth demands experiment, application, and verifiable consequences in human experience, Peirce would hold. The close relationship between early pragmatism and British Utilitarianism is evidenced by the fact that Peirce dedicated his book, *Pragmatism*, to John Stuart Mill.

d. William James (1842-1910) extended the new philosophy, pursuing lines of thought not developed or entirely approved by his colleague, Peirce. He conceived of pragmatism as a "method for settling philosophical disputes." The empirical attitude directed him to consider practical consequences and particulars in place of abstractions and universals. Whatever ideas actually worked or had contemporary "cash value" were true. His opposition to a priori judgments and to Calvinistic determinism is clearly seen in his admonition that men ought to assume freedom and get to work. Where absolutes had been, James substituted a pluralism of ideas whose value was to be proven by pragmatic test.

e. John Dewey (1859-1952) reaffirmed the empirical character of the new philosophy and further developed its tenets. It is commonly agreed that Dewey was the major spokesman for this school, synthesizing the data developed by others, applying the principles of pragmatism to every phase of human existence, and evolving a complete system of thought. Tribute should also be paid to George H. Mead (1863-1931), another one of the founders of pragmatism, but John Dewey was clearly the master architect.

Dewey held that the practice by philosophy of consistently basing its concepts on fixed principles could be traced back to the ancient Greeks. He proposed a reconstruction of philosophy, instituting approaches that were experiential, experimental, or as he preferred to call his view, instrumental. His metaphysics, regarded as very inadequate by classical philosophers, called for an emphasis on human experiences in continuity, implying an interaction with the present environment. Moral theory, he held, could not be based on a fixed goal, since no two ethical situations were the same. We should recognize a "plurality of goals," and furthermore, erase the false distinction between goals that are termed intrinsic and extrinsic.

The very nature of pragmatism demanded that it be tested for consequences or repudiate itself. Dewey chose to apply the newly-

discovered philosophy to the field of education. He viewed traditionalism as a system of questionable postulates promoting the memoriz-
ing of a historically-fixed body of subject matter, separating doing and
knowing. Its pattern of ethics and behavior was defended by adults in
authority in order to preserve the *status quo*. And the institutions of
learning were removed from their society which made the curricula
unrelated to real life, said Dewey.

2. *The Philosophy of Pragmatism*

The positions held by this school of thought have already been
sketched or inferred in the treatment of the views of its founders. It
is, nevertheless, necessary to state and define, in an organized manner, the system as it is today. For maximum clarity, the outline of general philosophy, employed in other chapters, will be followed.

a. *The Metaphysics of Pragmatism*

To the question, "What is real?" pragmatism does not offer the
historical answers, involving a concept of something predesigned, permanent, and unchanging. The basic consideration is not reason, concrete things, or mental realities. Rather, the key which connects all of
the preceding is experience. This master criterion is concerned with
the here and now and serves to relate men to ideas and things.

In contrast to the ontological position of realism and of idealism,
the experienced-centered philosophy of pragmatism emphasizes
change. Everything is conceived as being in process but not toward
pre-established ends; rather towards ends-in-view which eventually
become means to further ends-in-view. Experience itself is a flow,
plural in number, and dynamic in character. Pragmatic theory, at this
point, demonstrates a close relationship to the ancient philosophy of
the Greek, Heraclitus (535?-475?). Credence is also supplied to the
charge that pragmatism is allied with some modern theories of evolution, although there may be no "necessary" connection.

The pragmatist's concept of mind is, perhaps, best understood at
this juncture. The mind is not a cosmic abstraction which operates
separately from the human body. However, it is not an organ or

object. It is the cultivated ability of man to relate his experiences so that the latter confer certain advantages—for example, the power to communicate with other people. Mind, then, is a function of man, which necessarily evolved to aid man in adjustment and survival.

b. *The Logic and Epistemology of Pragmatism*

The preceding discussion dealing with the concept of mind is transitional to a treatment of pragmatic epistemology. Since mind is active, relating man to his world, it serves to provide him with information. As man interacts with ideas and things, he makes knowledge for himself; he does not discover it. Intelligence is necessary in the process of interacting and creating. The greater the application of human intelligence the more likelihood there is that real problems will be located and solved, the higher probability that knowledge will be received, and that human happiness will be increased.

Closely allied with the notions of mind and intelligence is that of truth. Like, mind, truth is active. Truth employs the knowledge we have received applying it to life's difficulties and directing us towards desirable solutions. What we perceive as truth must be proven as workable and to yield satisfactory results. Any idea found to be inadequate by this standard may be assumed to be false. To answer the question, "What is truth?" pragmatists simply point to desirable consequences.

c. *The Axiology of Pragmatism*

It should be obvious that if the metaphysics of pragmatism are the changing experiences of life, and if truth is created by the individual, values must be relative and primarily temporal. For the pure pragmatist there are no universals and no dogmatic principles of supernatural origin. On the contrary, values are developed through experiences and intelligent deliberation. Further, we must guard against drawing a sharp distinction between means as instrumental and ends as intrinsic, since in actual experience these two often reverse themselves.

The pragmatic theory of value clearly implies that both ethics, personal and social, and aesthetics, according to this school of thought, are individual, relative, and the products of human growth and interaction. Right and good arise from personal and social experiences when they are tested by intelligent application. Art, like ethics, is not handed down by certain authorities to each new generation. Instead, it is part of life itself, and its standards of value depend on the degree to which it enriches one's experience. These are the answers to the pragmatist's questions of "What is good?" and "What is beauty?"

One very important and fundamental value to pragmatists in general is that of democracy. Dewey insisted that the task of democracy was to develop human freedom, character, and intelligence. He asserted not only the importance of democracy for all people but that such a principle of life, which at first developed naturally, must now be maintained by intelligent effort.[5]

C. PROGRESSIVISM IN EDUCATION

Pragmatism is the general philosophy, a groundwork of basic assumptions, and progressivism is the counterpart in educational theory. The two terms are often confused because of the similarity of content. There is no closer degree of relationship between schools of general and educational philosophy than exists between pragmatism and progressivism. Here is a case where a theory of education is clearly deduced from a school of general philosophy.

1. Progressivist Educational Philosophy

It has already been pointed out that pragmatism holds to a metaphysical position involving the concept of experience. Progressivism fully accepts this base and holds that human beings learn through experiences that are physical and/or mental. Similarly, the emphasis is on present and personal activities and not on previous experiences of other people. Such an emphasis is in agreement with pragmatism's principle of change, since change is the very nature of human experi-

---

5. John Dewey, "Creative Democracy, the Task Before Us" in *Classic American Philosophers*, by Max Harold Fisch (New York: Appleton-Century-Crofts, 1951).

ence. Human experiences, however, are not valuable in and of themselves. The mind is to develop the ability to relate them and become
even more intelligent and so aid the individual in the pursuit of real
happiness, here and now.

Progressivism endorses the concept of truth enunciated by pragmatism. Truth is dynamic and relative. Both truth and knowledge are
altered by changing situations. The criterion of truth is still consequences. Progressivism agrees with John Locke in denying the theory
of innate ideas.

Values, such as the practice of democracy, must be created, not
discovered. Like truth, values are personal and dynamic. They are
also relative and developmental.

2. The Principles of Applied Progressivism

Eventually, the question must be answered, "What is the recom-
mended program by this educational philosophy when applied to a
real teaching-learning situation?" Here is the answer, presented in the
form of principles and practices:

a. The Place of the Teacher

The teacher's task is to guide the children's activities and to
seek to provide the best possible environment for learning. As a guide,
he is never obtrusive, always very democratic, ever respecting the
natural rights of all. He employs the psychological approach to the
organization of subject matter, remembering that the task of providing
motivation is more important than the dispensing of information.

b. The Place of the Child

At the center of the learning situation is the child as an individual, different from every other child, but with certain common interests and goals. The entire child, mind, body, and his total society,
in and out of the classroom, are involved and affect how he learns. He
should have freedom to discover truth and to develop knowledge for
himself. To every stimulus he responds as a whole person.

c. The Place of Subject Matter

The content should be like life itself, not compartmentalized, but overlapping, with each area contributing to every other area of learning. Planning the activities of the classroom should be a joint enterprise, involving both students and teachers. The classroom should encompass the world as the curiosity, maturation level, and growing interest of the pupils may demand. As far as possible, the classroom should be a miniature of the good life outside and should be closely related to real living. Teaching which involves group learning, audio-visual aids, field trips, and project-unit type organization of subject matter seems to serve these goals best.

d. The Place of Society

The school is an institution of society, not somehow separated, but involved in social experiences, and contributing to the on-going activity of its supporting community. A good school will recognize this close relationship, and seek both to reflect the norms of society and to direct its future toward greater human happiness. The schools should seek to prepare the youth for leadership, responsibility, and democratic living.

D. EVALUATION AND CRITICISM

No other philosophy of education has been attacked as often or as vigorously as progressivism. Most, if not all, opposing philosophies saw it as a threat to their positions. Religionists, especially, viewed progressivism as godless and certain to undermine faith, accepted moral practices, and social patterns. A recent critic with more wit than understanding prepared an album of records entitled, "Warmed over Rickover Leftovers," one platter of which paraphrased a popular song with, "Hang Down Your Head, John Dewey."

Most of the serious protests seemed to fall into one of the following areas:

1. Metaphysical Position

The proponents of pragmatism offer what has often been termed a very inadequate theory of metaphysics. The key word for both pragmatism and progressivism is "experience," which fails to tell us anything about the nature of ultimate reality. This area was the first concern of the older and historical systems of philosophy.

2. The Concept of Truth

Truth, according to pragmatism, can be made by anyone and proven simply by observing the consequences. This suggests that truth is not held in very high regard. Classical philosophers had maintained that truth, including logical means for its discovery and related epistemology, were fundamental considerations. Further, many great truths are valuable in themselves and offer no possibility of empirical verification.

3. The Concept of Mind

As in the case of truth, pragmatists seem to hold mind in low regard. Where once mind was thought to have an affinity with the universe, it has now been reduced to an ability to adjust to one's environment and a means to obtain physical needs. Instead of rationality being the goal of human existence, it is now the means of survival.

4. Axiological Position

Pragmatism, at this point, is charged with contradicting itself. If all values are relative and nothing is permanent, then the so-called truths and values of pragmatism are open to question. Perhaps they, too, are no longer valid.

5. The Emphasis on the Present

Pragmatism is accused of placing its heaviest emphasis on contemporary activities. The demand for experiences in continuity clearly contributes to this position. Yet history has taught many lessons, including the greater value of the more stable, remote goals as contrasted with the activities of the present.

6. *The Relationship to Darwinism*

Many people have assumed a "necessary" and close relationship between pragmatism and Darwin's theory of creative evolution. As a result, progressivism's emphasis on development, change, and adjustment has been regarded by some, especially orthodox religionists, as evil. It should be pointed out that one may be a pragmatist and not an evolutionist, and also that there are a variety of views on the theory of evolution itself.

7. *Subject Matter Versus Adjustment*

The most frequently heard criticism of progressivism is that there is insufficient concern for concrete subject matter. It is held that instead of providing the students with a genuine education, the educators use the time and facilities to foster lesser goals of personal and social adjustment. In defense, the progressive educators often cite the results of their eight-year study.[6]

8. *The Place of the Teacher*

While several of the major educational philosophies emphasize to varying degrees, the importance of the teacher, progressivism appears to position the teacher on the periphery of the learning situation. The charge is that if the teacher is only a guide and friend, then the supporting philosophy in practice negates the maturity, knowledge, and wisdom of an instructor.

9. *The Problem of Misinterpretation*

Although progressivism is not particularly difficult to comprehend, there have been many people who have almost intentionally misconstrued some of its tenets. The concepts of child-centeredness and freedom have sometimes been used by teachers as excuses for doing as little as possible, and by ultra-modern parents as reasons for abdicating their responsibility toward their children.

---

6. W. M. Aiken, "The Story of the Eight-year Study," Ernest O. Melby and Morten Puner, eds., *Freedom and Public Education.*

10. *Outer Man Versus Inner Man*

Similarities between progressivism and existentialism are in many instances not as real as a superficial view would make them appear. One fundamental and major criticism of both pragmatism and progressivism by the existentialists is that the former emphasizes personal and social development while ignoring the inner man. Personal identity is prior to personal adjustment.

11. *The Roots of Progressivism*

The fact that progressivism rose as a reaction to other philosophies, especially traditionalism, is not to its credit. Its critics say that the approach of this school in education is primarily negative in character.

FURTHER READING

Aiken, W. M. "The Story of the Eight Year Study," *Freedom and Public Education,* Melby, Ernest O. and Morten Puner (editors). New York: Harper and Row, 1942.

Bayles, Ernest E. *Pragmatism in Education.* New York: Harper and Row, Publishers, 1966.

Brubacher, John S. *A History of the Problems of Education* (2nd ed.). New York: McGraw-Hill Book Company, 1966.

Butler, J. Donald. *Four Philosophies and Their Practice in Education and Religion.* New York: Harper and Row, Publishers, 1968.

Childs, John L. *American Pragmatism and Education.* New York: Henry Holt and Company, 1956.

Childs, John L. *Education and the Philosophy of Experimentalism.* New York: The Century Company, 1931.

Davis, Elwood C. *Philosophies Fashion Physical Education.* Dubuque, Iowa: William C. Brown, Publishers, 1963.

Dewey, John. "Creative Democracy, the Task Before Us," *Classic American Philosophers,* Max Harold Fisch. New York: Appleton-Century-Crofts, 1951.

Dewey, John. *Democracy and Education.* New York: The Macmillan Company. 1916.

Dewey, John. *Experience and Education.* New York: The Macmillan Company, 1951.

Dewey, John. *Reconstruction in Philosophy.* London: University of London Press, 1921.

Frankena, William F. *Three Historical Philosophies of Education*. Chicago: Scott, Foresman and Company, 1965.

Johnson, Henry C., Jr. "Progressive Education: A Case of Arrested Development?" *Educational Theory*, Vol. XV, No. 3 (July, 1965), pp. 188-197.

Lee, Gordon C. *Education and Democratic Ideals*. New York: Harcourt, Brace and World, 1965.

Little, Charles E. *Quintilian, the Schoolmaster*. Vol. I. Nashville, Tennessee: The Peabody Press, 1951.

Wahlquish, John T. *The Philosophy of American Education*. New York: The Ronald Press, 1942.

Weber, Christian O. *Basic Philosophies of Education*. New York: Holt, Rinehart and Winston, 1966.

Wynne, John Peter. *Philosophies of Education*. New York: Prentice-Hall, Inc., 1947.

"An Experimentalist's Approach to Education," a film. New Film Service, Indiana University, Bloomington, Indiana.

Chapter IV

ESSENTIALISM,
The Ideal Elements

As an organized body of educational ideas, essentialism is a relatively new addition to the field. However, the concepts which comprise this school of thought are as old as Greek philosophy itself. This educational theory first appeared in organized form in the United States as the "conservative view" in the 1930's. The term, conservative, meaning void of extremes, seemed to imply that it did not want to be identified with the successors of dogmatic puritanism on one hand or the advocates of child-freedom on the other. The call by one of its early supporters, Professor Fuller of the University of Chicago, for a philosophy of the "middle ground," apparently a point between traditionalism and progressivism, adds to the contention that it was and is a separate school of thought. It should not be confused with intellectual discipline or with any other view, which, from certain perspectives, might be referred to as conservative.

A. IDEALISM AS A BASIC PHILOSOPHY

Essentialism has been rightly called the most eclectic of all the schools of educational thought. Although it is true that it is characterized by a degree of religious philosophy, and certainly by both ancient and modern views of realism, there is a dominance of idealism in both the foundational assumptions and in the application to educational practices. Since the relationship of realism to education is treated elsewhere in this volume, only the place of idealism will be discussed here.

1. *Historical Foundations of Idealism*

The philosophers of most schools of general and educational thought like to refer in their writings to the great thinkers of ancient Greece. Then they attempt to trace the development of their theories from those ancient days to the present. Through its historical relationship to idealism, essentialism is more justified in doing this than are some of the other schools of educational philosophy, even though the strength of the present bond between idealism and essentialism is currently in question. Returning to idealism as a general philosophy, we will begin our discussion with Plato, a student of Socrates.

a. *Plato (427-347 B.C.)*

Plato posed a number of questions which have served to direct the course of Western thought. One such question was to do with the contradictory fact of permanency in the midst of constant change in a world of apparent order. Plato's answer was to divide the world into two realms, one of changing particulars such as earth, water, and individual men; the other of universals—ideas of forms of things that did not change. For every particular there was a universal. But for some universals such as goodness, beauty, and essence there were no corresponding particulars. These were, nevertheless, absolute realities. This doctrine of ideas, as it is commonly termed, answered for Plato the question of permanency versus change and emphasized the concept that the realm of ideas was ultimate and of paramount importance. What is probably even more important to the teacher is the fact that an educational program based on Platonic idealism would emphasize the priority of ideas over matter, the importance of developing human virtues such as wisdom, temperance, courage, and justice, the existence of a degree of conservatism and absolutism in education, and the need for mental acumen in the learners in order to comprehend the significance of these universals.

b. *Immanuel Kant (1724-1804)*

The years from Plato to Immanuel Kant contain many important figures of which one of the most outstanding was the German philosopher-mathematician, Gottfried Wilhelm von Leibnitz (1646-1716). His proximity in time to Immanuel Kant permits only a passing mention of him here. He conceived of the world as a unity of individual beings all organized according to a "pre-established harmony." The idealism of Leibnitz is obvious and his importance as a forerunner of Immanuel Kant is an accepted fact.

Königsberg, Germany was the life-center for Kant. It was here he was born, attended university, lectured for many years in a great variety of subjects, and presented in 1781 his first major work, the *Critique of Pure Reason*. He has since been regarded as one of the greatest thinkers of all time.

Kant was a student of human reason and attempted to relate to human thought such concepts as sensation, perception, and experience in categories of time and space. His investigations led him to ascribe to the existence of certain universal laws which man has the duty and freedom to choose to obey, the belief in an immortal human soul which must become holy, and in the necessity for the existence of God. In summary, Kantian idealism assigns special significance to ideas, thought, the self, freedom of choice, to certain religious doctrines such as the existence of eternal verities, and the unity of the whole universal plan. Philosophers and educators ever since have paid homage to Kant and built on the foundation he laid. One of these, which may be of interest to many students, was George Hegel (1770-1831), remembered for his highly abstract, absolute idealism. The same spirit is seen in the works of the American philosopher, Josiah Royce (1855-1916), and in the essays of Ralph Waldo Emerson (1803-1882), sometimes called "the American Pestalozzi."

2. Idealism as a System of Philosophy

For several reasons, the presentation of a brief summary of idealism is no easy task. Since Plato there have appeared many different types of idealism and a variety of interpretations by different authors. Furthermore, there are aspects of idealism which resemble the principles of realism, and efforts to simplify the tenets of either school of thought often serve to emphasize those similarities rather than the differences. What follows here is a brief treatment of the commonly accepted position of idealism with regard to the three major areas of general philosophy.

a. *Metaphysical Position*

Idealism answers the question, "What is real?" by offering a concept of the self and the mind as prime reality. Descartes gave evidence of the self when he said, "I think, therefore I am." This self is, furthermore, spiritual, mental, and representative of a community and of the whole universe. Idealism sees the world as an intelligible, predetermined order to which man as the self must learn to conform. Over all is God, spiritual and mental, and also infinite. This last accounts in part for the strong religious flavor found in some interpretations of idealism.

b. *Epistemology and Logic*

Knowledge of the self is fundamental here, but the process of obtaining this information varies among idealists. Is the self known by a direct observation of itself or is this knowledge gleaned from some inference—such as thought? In any event all knowledge is part of the universal whole so that every part is related to every other and can only be understood as such. Truth is part of the fabric of the universe; it is a series of orderly and systematic relationships. Furthermore, truth is something men discover; they do not create it.

The emphasis on unity and wholeness which is so evident in the epistemology of idealism is also seen in the idealistic theory of logic. Both deductive and inductive logic are admitted as tools of the mind for the interpretation of data. Idealism holds that there is an established body of generally accepted information. Such truths need no defense. Truth comes through discovery and is related to every other aspect of human knowledge.

c. *Concepts in Axiology*

The idealist answers the question, "What is Value?" by stating that values, like a Platonic universal, have real existence. Values are, in a sense, inherited; yet each individual must work out his own relationship to them. They are not dogmas, as imposed by traditionalism; rather they are laws and standards which we determine in the exercise of our rights. In sum, the self and the mind, operating logically and within the bounds of human freedom, will enlarge the understanding, recognize relationships, and eventually accept the good and the beautiful as part of a universal and harmonious pattern.

B. ESSENTIALISM, THE EDUCATIONAL THEORY

Reference was made in the preceding paragraphs to the fact that essentialism rose as a protest to the presumed extremes of progressivism. The criticisms by these conservatives in the 1930's may be summarized as follows:

> Goals: In our concern for the personal, social, and vocational, we have forgotten to develop the intellect.
> Teachers: The demand for a democratic classroom has moved the instructor to a position of minor importance, bringing about a decline in the quality of education.
> Pupils: An over-emphasis on the interests, needs, and wishes of the pupils has failed to help the slow learners and has deprived the more precocious pupils of a proper education. Further, teachers should not only emphasize pupil adjustment to contemporary modern life, but to something higher and more stable.
> Curriculum: The generally accepted subjects of academic study have been largely by-passed in favor of easier material, which often is only trivia.
> Society: Educators have committed a grave injustice to American society in failing to develop the potential of the pupils academically and to inculcate that heritage of proven values which makes for good men and truly great community.

1. *The Development of Essentialism*

Fragments of and implications favoring essentialism can be found in the writings of philosophers and educators from the Greek period to the present. Also, wherever there were idealists, and to a lesser degree, realists, there appeared statements concerning education that were clearly conservative. For evidence one only has to read from Plato himself, or from the Englishman, John Locke (1632-1704). German contributors include not only Immanuel Kant, who was discussed previously, but also Johann Friedrick Herbart (1776-1841). The best-known American supporter prior to the actual founding of an essentialist's organization was William T. Harris, Hegelian idealist, known for his leadership in Saint Louis, and later as United States Commissioner of Education. With such favor and support, one may wonder why essentialism was so tardy in its development in the American community. The answer reminds one of the law of the pendulum—first excluded by the dogmatism of traditionalism, it was later overshadowed by the more attractive promises of progressivism.

Organized American essentialism is dated from a meeting held in Atlantic City, New Jersey, in 1938, when "The Essentialist's Committee for the Advancement of Education" came into being. The "Committee," as it later became known, had no intent of declaring war on progressivism, but this was the interpretation by some people. The following excerpt from an article by this author adds further details:

> Seven members comprised the committee when it was originated in 1938. They were the chairman, F. Alden Shaw, headmaster of the Detroit Country Day School; Guy M. Whipple, psychologist and editor of elementary school books; Louis Shores, Milton L. Shane, Michael Demiaschkevich (who in 1935 suggested the term "Essentialist") of George Peabody College for Teachers; Walter H. Ryle, President of Northeast Missouri State Teachers College; and Bagley, who was recognized as the leading spokesman of the essentialists—even more so than John Dewey was of the progressives. Other leading names in American education eventually became associated with essentialism, two of the most noteworthy being Isaac I. Kandel, famous for his laying of the groundwork for studies in comparative education, and Robert Ulich, philosopher and historian at Harvard University.[1]

The Committee quietly continued its work in the years which followed. While the Great Depression and World War II weakened the cause of progressivism, essentialism as an educational theory was fostered. The death of Bagley in 1946 was a severe blow which rendered the Committee inactive, but it did not deter the militant upward movement of the persistent ideas which this school promoted.

---

1. William H. Howick, "Progressivism Versus Essentialism in Teacher Education," *Educational Quest,* Vol. XIII, No. 1, Winter, 1969, pp. 21-28.

Now the world has entered a new era, one particularly characterized by a technological race between the United States and the Soviet Union. The demand for the well-educated, the thinking man, has grown stronger. And essentialism under the simple banner of "modern education" has become a philosophy demanding the consideration of every rational person. The orbiting of the first early satellite, the Russian Sputnik, in 1957 added impetus to the cause for essentialism. Best known among its supporters today are J. Donald Butler, seminarian, James Bryant Conant, former president of Harvard University, and William W. Brickman, noted editor of educational periodicals.

2. The Principles of Essentialism

The idealist-essentialist relationship is most easily understood in connection with specific educational topics, as follows:

a. The teacher is the center of the educative process. He places great importance on the understanding of ideas as models of perfection which are, therefore, ideals to accept and follow. The proven essentials of a proper education for youth in a changing society include a knowledge of great leaders and events which have made a difference in the course of history

His attitude is that required by a democratic society, which does not imply either teacher-dominion or pupil permissiveness. The teacher is to assume the initiative, set the climate of the classroom, and select and interpret the essentials of the learning process. Such a task requires teachers who are well qualified academically, emotionally stable, and with a genuine appreciation of the nature of human growth and development. Keeping good records is part of his professional task. He seeks to motivate his students to learn by his own example and to control them by the intelligent use of rewards and penalties.

b. The pupil is important in the learning process, subordinated only by his lack of knowing and living. He is to be intelligently submissive, meanwhile searching for knowledge and understanding in order to qualify for his rightful place in adult society. Success in life requires him to overcome his own lack of interest, and to develop virtues of self-control, self-dependency, and self-discipline. He must

understand   the value of proper authority and adult direction in
achieving goals.

c. The curriculum of essentialism would include the time tested
subjects which have already proven their value to the democratic
community. Contrary to some interpreters the student would study
his environment, the laws of nature, and science as contributors to
personal happiness and nobler living. Less important areas, not regarded as "essential" should be added only when there is assurance
that the established subjects will not be affected adversely.

d. The methods employed by the essentialist teacher would
fall in an area midway between the rigid procedure of assignment,
memorization, and recitation of old-fashioned traditionalism, and the
directionless freedom of modern progressivism. The teacher, mainly by
lecture and guided discussion, sees that the pupil adds to his store of
true knowledge, and the pupil's task is to apply himself as diligently
as he will to this undertaking. Some learning can be made interesting
and some cannot. Certain material has present and practical value
while other knowledge is deposited in the mind for use in achieving
distant goals. Assigning specific areas for study is very often necessary
and some learning may be obtained only by purposeful memorization.
But superior to ordinary rote-learning is a profound understanding of
the ideas involved, a kind of "conceptualization." Not all knowledge
can be learning by experience or through a study of problems. Much
of what we learn is by its nature abstract and idea-istic. Our untested,
personal experiences should not be the core of the curriculum. Often
they serve only to support higher learning involving thought and contemplation. Besides, thinking is an experience itself, one without which
no academic learning ever takes place.

e. The relationship of the essentialist school to society has never
been well-developed by the proponents of this position. Clearly, the
essentialists are democratic in practice and attitude both in the classroom and in the community at large. However, the task of the American school here would seem to be that of conserving and reinforcing
those personal and social virtues which time has proven to be essential for the continuance of an organized society. Further search and
evaluation will reveal added essentials which the schools in turn

should teach to the young and thus make for social progress. The improvement of society must necessarily be gradual, never brought about by massive government welfare programs which only suppress human virtues such as self-dependence and self-sufficiency, and result in a loss of selfhood and individualism.

C. EVALUATION AND CRITICISM

Essentialism as a philosophy of education has been the object of criticism ever since the organization of the "Essentialist's Committee" in 1938. The critics have often been social reconstructionists, but more frequently, they have been advocates of progressivism in education. A brief statement of each accusation follows:

1. Essentialism is undemocratic in its overemphasis on the place of adults and the need for conservation of the culture. Its educational program requires that an organization be set up by adults, involving certain ideas which students must eventually accept and standards which they must attain. The supporters seem to be saying that this is right because it has always been right.

2. This position leads toward cultural lag. Conservatism, by its nature, retards the development of both the individual and the society. Although essentialism as a middle-of-the-road philosophy is better than that of traditionalism with its determinism and extreme demands for conformity, it does not go far enough.

3. There might very well be a contradiction between the fundamental theory and actual practice of the essentialist teacher. The theory emphasizes mind, ideas, self, and the need to develop independence and self-sufficiency, while in practice there appears to be considerable pressure on the pupil to give willing acceptance to what is taught.

4. The final charge is that the social and cultural heritage is exalted and lauded as if it had some intrinsic value all of its own. The culture, say the critics, is a dynamic force involving changing people in a changing society.

FURTHER READING

Bagley, William C. "The Case for Essentialism in Education," *The Journal of the National Education Association*, Vol. XXX (October, 1941), pp. 201-202.

Bagley, William C. *Education and Emergent Man*. New York: The Ronald Press, 1934.

Bagley, William C. "An Essentialist's Platform for the Advancement of American Education," *Educational Administration and Supervision,* Vol. XXIV (April, 1938), pp. 241-256.

Bagley, William C. "Just What Is the Crux of the Conflict Between Progressives and the Essentialists?" *Educational Administration and Supervision,* Vol. XXVI (September, 1940), pp. 508-511.

Bode, Boyd H. *Progressive Education at the Crossroads*. Chicago: Newson and Company, 1938.

Brameld, Theodore. *Patterns of Educational Philosophy*. New York: World Book Company, 1950.

Brameld, Theodore. *Philosophies of Education in Cultural Perspective*. New York: The Dryden Press, Inc., 1955.

Brickman, William W. "A Call to Essentialists," *School and Society,* Vol. LXXIX (March 20, 1954), pp. 91-92.

Brickman, William W. "Essentialism Ten Years After," *School and Society,* Vol. LXVII (May 15, 1948), pp. 361-362.

Butler, J. Donald, *Idealism in Education*. New York: Harper and Row, Publishers, 1966.

Callahan, Raymond E. *An Introduction to Education in American Society* (2nd ed.). New York: Alfred A. Knopf, Publisher, 1960.

Chambers, Gurney. "Educational Essentialism Thirty Years After," *School and Society,* Vol. XCVII, No. 2314 (January, 1969), pp. 14-16.

Cremin, Lawrence A. *The Transformation of the School: Progressivism in American Education*. New York: Alfred A. Knopf, Publisher, 1962.

Davis, Elwood C. *Philosophies Fashion Physical Education*. Dubuque, Iowa: William C. Brown, Publishers, 1963.

Demiashkevich, Michael. *An Introduction to the Philosophy of Education*. New York: American Book Company, 1935.

Harvard Committe. The Report of *General Education in a Free Society*. Cambridge, Massachusetts: Harvard University Press, 1945.

Hearn, Edell M. "William Chandler Bagley," *Kappa Delta Pi Record,* Vol. IV, No. 1 (October, 1967), pp. 19-23.

Howick, William H. "Progressivism Versus Essentialism in Teacher Education," *Educational Quest,* Vol. XIII, No. 1 (Winter, 1969), pp. 21-28.

Kandel, Isaac L. *William Chandler Bagley*. Columbia University, New York: Teachers College Publications, 1961.

Mason, Robert E. *Educational Ideals in American Society*. Boston: Allyn and Bacon, Inc., 1960.

Moelman, Arthur B. "William C. Bagley, Master Teacher," *The Nation's Schools,* Vol. XXXVIII (October, 1956), p. 19.

Ulich, Robert. *Fundamentals of Democratic Education*. New York: American Book Company, 1940.

Chapter V

CLASSICAL REALISM,
The Permanency of the Perennial

The name assigned by educational philosophers to this school of thought indicates quite clearly its general position. It is based primarily on that organized body of concepts known as realism, but there is admittedly a considerable amount of idealism, too. The term, "classical," implies that the proponents draw heavily on the literature written a long time ago. Some philosophers prefer to call this school by the name, "perennialism," in order to emphasize the belief that this philosophy is based on ideas that will never die. Other titles such as Neo-Scholasticism and Neo-Thomism are used to indicate particular areas of emphasis and divisions within this major school of thought. Regardless of the name employed to refer to this body of ideas, all its supporters would like to see the present pattern of Western culture, with its empiricism and scientism, replaced by one involving the enduring classical and philosophical principles.

A. THE HISTORICAL AND PHILOSOPHICAL BASIS

Classical realism, more than any other school of educational thought, is anchored to the past. This deep respect for historical background and the belief that we should somehow redirect modern civilization so as to cause it to conform eventually to the pattern set down by certain thinkers of long ago, have motivated some opponents of this school to label it "regressive." Just how far back these educator-philosophers would go, varies, but it is generally agreed that the basis must include the contributions of the Greek democratic state, especially those prior to 146 B.C.

1. The Greek Fountainhead

Classical Greek philosophy was born just across the Aegean Sea from Athens at a place called Miletus in Asia Minor. The first important philosophers of the Western World did their work there beginning with Thales at approximately 600 B.C. Some of the great questions which occupied the minds of these philosopher-scientists were, "What is the essence or basic 'stuff' of the universe?" "How can change be explained?" "What makes for the apparent permanence of things?" At a little later date the questions moved from the cosmological to the epistemological, and thence to a concern for human values. At this point some of the questions were, "What is truth?" and "What is beauty?"

It should be admitted that the ancient Greeks did not originate all of their concepts. Apparently they borrowed to some degree from other civilizations, especially from India, Babylonia, and Egypt. Further, it must not be assumed that these great Greek philosophers found satisfactory answers to all their questions, or even that the answers which they regarded as acceptable then have proven to be examples of permanent truth today. On the contrary, a number of solutions offered by thinkers of this period to their problems have been found to be false. What, then, is the importance of their philosophies? It is not so much their answers but their profound questions which have directed the course of Western civilization.

Socrates (469-399 B.C.) is historically significant here, since he was the human pivot which redirected philosophical inquiry away from the outer world and towards a consideration of man himself. His method of teaching, that of using the right questions to lead the student to the discovery of the right answers already determined by the teacher, is noteworthy. Likewise, Socrates' student, Plato, is important as a major contributor to the Greek Fountainhead of Knowledge, and has been treated elsewhere in this work.

a. Aristotle (384-322 B.C.) occupies the most prominent place of all with regard to the historical foundations of classical realism. His philosophy is best presented for our purposes in the following order:

(1) Logic, to Aristotle, was an area of major importance involving a study of ideas, as represented by words, in relationship to each other. In order to properly analyze language he classified all known concepts into what he termed "categories." Using the syllogism he was then able to deal with scientific discourse and to formulate proofs in metaphysics and axiology.

(2) Axiology in the writings of Aristotle focuses its attention chiefly on the good man, the good state, and the values of art and music. His theory of ethics has been called "teleological," since the concern is always with the fulfillment of ends, instrumental and intrinsic. A thing is good when it achieves the end peculiar to it. In the case of man, the ultimate good is happiness, which is attained through reason. Vice, the opposite of good, results when man loses rational control of his passions and strays too far from the "golden mean," that point of virtue between two extremes.

Aristotle's theory of the good state is consistent with that of a good man. The state also exists for a distinctive purpose, namely to foster moral and intellectual fulfillment. An aristocracy, that is, administration by the select few, would provide the environment most conducive to the contemplation necessary for human happiness.

The value of art lies in the fact that it communicates knowledge about nature to man. According to this cognitive theory, art tends to illustrate the existence of its universal concept, and the contemplation of it makes for pleasure and happiness. Music of the right kind is especially important in the development of good character in the young.

(3) Metaphysics to Aristotle is the science of "first philosophy." Its abstractions go beyond any knowledge obtained by mere sense experience, however reliable the latter may be. Metaphysical studies lead to true wisdom, because they deal with underlying causes and principles which constitute true reality. The paramount concern of metaphysics is the essence, the universal, or form of anything, man or object. Such reasoning led Aristotle to distinguish between matter as concrete and known by the senses, and the corresponding form of each thing. This theory of forms, or universals, solved for both Plato

and Aristotle the historic problem of permanence in the midst of change. It is the matter which we see that changes while the universal remains unaltered. At this point Plato and Aristotle disagree and proceed along different routes. While Plato had separated the universals into a remote realm of their own, his student maintained that a universal was somehow embedded in every particular object. Such an explanation was necessary, held Aristotle, in order for individual things to have any value and to make them objects of scientific study. This union of form and matter has been given a special name, that of "hylomorphism." The doctrine largely accounts for the description of Aristotle's philosophy as animistic in which everything is striving to move from its "potentiality" to "actuality" in achieving its highest end. Overall is the prior cause for all change and motion, an Unmoved Mover. To Aristotle such a prior actuality was necessary not for theological purposes but for scientific ones. The Unmoved Mover was in no sense a creator and did not determine the future of the universe. It was capable of causing change and motion in much the same way that a lover affects his beloved simply by attraction.

b. Aristotle's Unmoved Mover was interpreted in the *Summa Theologica* of Saint Thomas Aquinas (1225-1274), Angelic Doctor of the University of Paris, as the God of Christianity. This interpretation was reaffirmed by the church in the historic Council of Trent (1545-1563). The view of universals as having real existence became vital to the dogmas of the church. They were basic to the proofs for the realities of sin, faith, salvation, and eternity as well as God Himself. Aquinas is still regarded as the greatest of the Scholastics, since he succeeded in synthesizing Greek philosophy with its emphasis on reason, and Christian doctrine based on faith.

As may be expected, not everyone agreed with Aristotle's theory of universals. Of note here is the function served by Roscellinus (1050-1125), once a teacher of the great Abelard. Roscellinus rejected the notion that universals have real existence. He held that names applied to universals were mere terms, and did not refer to anything. Such a position would have left man with nothing but particulars. Abelard (1079-1142) offered a more moderate position by suggesting that since we observe the similarities among objects of the same kind, we tend to abstract the universal from the particular. Thinkers of that day generally accepted the moderate realism of Abelard, but the effect was nevertheless to weaken the importance of abstract universals and to direct the attention of the scientifically inclined toward a consideration of the particular objects themselves. Here, at these historic crossroads, hold many thinkers, Western civilization considered its direction and then moved toward the new view of universals and objects. When men might have trod in the footsteps of Aristotle and followed philosophy, or after Aquinas, becoming religious and theological, they chose to discount universals and to emphasize the objective and the concrete. This error has led us to scientism, technology, empiricism, and secularism.

2. Realism as a System of Philosophy

Not all realists express themselves with the same emphasis and thus, not all can be referred to by exactly the same term. John Milton was a Humanistic Realist, Francis Bacon, a Scholastic Realist, and John Locke a Social Realist. There are Scholastic Realists who are Neo-Thomists, and then there are the views of modern Realism brought about by the acceptance of the nominalism of Roscellinus and the influence of Ockham (ca. 1280-1349).

Realism as a system of thought stems from the writings of Aristotle in particular. It began as a critique of and revolt against Platonic idealism. The fact that man's concept of the real has undergone modification during intervening centuries serves to complicate the task of understanding the positions held by this school.

a. Metaphysical Position

Reality to the classical realist is universal, abstract, and permanent. To understand reality one does not look from this realm to a Platonic world of ideas. Rather, reality is found by turning one's attention to the visible objects we encounter constantly. Like Aristotle, the classical realist is concerned with the essence, or nature of the object. Unlike the modern realist, he is not interested in the accidental characteristics of the matter which embodies the essence. Everything has its own essential nature. The essence of man is his ability to contemplate, so we say man's essence is to reason. We see man as a synthesis of body with form or essence. Not every man actualizes this end due to the absence of the proper conditions, in which case the potentiality remains latent. Neo-Thomists see this concept as one which promises righteousness and a future existence characterized by peace and controlled by pure actuality, God Himself. Not all realists, however, are ecclesiastical; some are lay perennialists who naturally deal with human affairs, past and present.

b. *Epistemological Position*

Truth to the classical realist is the conformity of thoughts to things as they are in their essence. One must not stop with a consideration of concrete objects but must contemplate that which comes "after" as implied by the Greek prefix "meta" in the word metaphysics. Truth is the product of logic and reason and is expressed in fundamental principles. Some obvious truths are "self-evident" and need no defense. Examples of this last point can be found by examining the minor premises of Aristotelian syllogisms.

Clearly, philosophy occupies the crowning position in any hierarchy of studies prepared by the classical realists. Philosophy deals with reality, with the unchanging and perennial. All other fields of learning are dependent and subordinate. Studies in the physical sciences occupy an especially inferior position, since they deal with the accidental characteristics of physical objects.

c. *Axiological Position*

Values like all the universals are permanently fixed. The supernatural is the source of all value for the Neo-Thomist. For the secular perennialist, values are permanently grounded in the fundamental purposes of the universe and await man's discovery.

Virtue is attained by striving to move from the material and potential toward the actual. The highest good for lay perennialists is the life of reason; for ecclesiastical perennialists this would be second only to becoming one with God. In either case the Aristotelian demand for happiness would be attained. Art, like virtue, is related to the attainment of actuality. The true artist represents essence by the use of symbols. He reproduces beauty, the goal of all aesthetics.

B. CLASSICAL REALISM AS A SCHOOL OF EDUCATIONAL PHILOSOPHY

The name, classical realism, may be employed to refer to either the supporting system of general philosophy or the corresponding school of educational thought. For some educators, the preferred term for the latter reference is perennialism. In the following discussion of educational theory, these two names will be used interchangeably.

1. Development to Modern Times

Realism as a system of general philosophy with implications for education survived the Dark Ages, the opposition of a powerful clergy, and the general ignorance of the people. Certain writers made significant contributions to the permanency of the ideas involved, and the most important are mentioned here.

Michel de Montaigne (1533-1592) was a noted French essayist. His writings, especially, "On Pedantry" and "On the Education of Children," mark him as a realist. An avid reader, and the owner of an unusually large library for his day, he became most familiar with the use of classical quotations. All of his works indicate that his greatest enjoyment came from his manipulation of ideas as he sought to relate them.

Contemporary with Montaigne was Richard Mulcaster (1530-1611), a teacher during the English Renaissance and headmaster of the famed Merchant-Taylors' School, and later of St. Paul's, both in London. Mulcaster's writings in education, "Positions," and "Elementaire," indicate the movement among realists toward the more practical and down-to-earth approach to education. There is still the deep admiration for language and ideas, and the insistence that all children read the better books, write well, know music, religion, and the theoretical basis for morality.

John Milton (1600-1674), once a school teacher but better known as a writer of essays, is grouped with Erasmus and Rabelais as a Humanistic Realist. The "Tractate on Education" is his best known work in that field. Although he laments the time that youth must spend learning Greek and Latin, he advocates their continuance and even the added study of other tongues such as Hebrew and Italian.

Eventually, Milton's student was to become familiar with all known areas of learning—mathematical, philosophical, scientific, literary, the arts, and, of course, religion, to mention most of them. Like other realists, Milton did not fail to ask that the student learn much about the past and develop his intellect and insights through a study of ideas.

The influence of Aristotle, Thomas Aquinas, and others, some of whom have just been mentioned here, has continued to modern times. John Henry Cardinal Newman (1801-1890) and the eminent French philosopher, Jacques Maritain, of the present century have been leading perennialists. Many more could be cited in a larger work than this.

Two contemporary Aristotelians are Robert Maynard Hutchins and Mortimer Adler. While developing their friendship these two men also developed their agreed concepts. Education to these writers is theoretical, that is, philosophical, intellectual, and concerned with wisdom for wisdom's sake. Hutchins, formerly a professor of law at Yale University, became president of the University of Chicago in 1929, and shortly thereafter Adler also joined the Chicago faculty. Meanwhile, John Erskine, professor at Columbia University, had developed a method of teaching honor students in literature by utilizing a selected list of great books. Hutchins and Adler further developed the concept and eventually founded the now well-known Great Books Foundation. The emphasis of this organization has been typically perennialist.

A further example of perennialism in practice is the program of studies offered by St. John's College, a private institution in Annapolis, Maryland. Hutchins, as a member of that College's Board of Trustees, persuaded the president, Stringfellow Barr, to organize the program so as to make it a modern version of the seven ancient liberal arts built upon a knowledge of the perennial ideas as contained in the great books. Since 1937, all students at St. John's have followed this single prescribed curriculum which promises to graduate them as properly educated adults. The education offered is liberal in the sense that it liberates the scholar from errors in thought, from ignorance and superstition. According to Mortimer Adler, it is "the only college in the world."

Perennialism has been kept alive for centuries by the Roman Catholic Church. The interpretations by Aquinas, especially in his *Summa Theologica,* of the writings of Aristotle have become the basis for church dogma. Its implications for learning have been the theory of education in Roman Catholic schools universally. Currently there is a significant rise in secular perennialism, and only time will reveal the effects on education as a whole.

2. *Educational Concepts*

Perennialists invariably discount all other systems of educational thought. The propositions of their opponents are mere opinions and have no real basis. True educational philosophy is a kind of universal which is known only by the purely rational approach. That which constitutes a proper education is singular, absolute, and universal.

a. *The Aims of Education*

For the classical realist the goal of education is the student's intellectual and moral development. In typical Aristotelian fashion, the learner is expected to actualize his potentiality. The ability to do so is embedded like a universal in every man in equal proportion so that under the proper conditions everyone is able to achieve this end. Such a goal rests fundamentally upon the concept that human nature is universally the same.

b. *The Curriculum*

The actualization of the learner's intellectual potential has been attained to a significant degree when he has made reason a habit. This ability to think clearly is essential for discovering truth. Education is a preparation for tomorrow through the acceptance of irrevocable truths—not through adjustment to changing particulars such as fellow men and society.

One must have something to reason about and the perennial problems and questions of the great thinkers of all time provide the necessary material. In order to study these permanent truths, the tools of learning, reading, writing, and arithmetic should be mastered during the elementary years. An appreciation of the great classics and for the fine arts should also be developed. At the secondary level the stress should be on a program of general education for all boys and girls. It should involve a study of foreign languages, including Greek and Latin with vigorous training in grammar, logic, rhetoric, and the principles of natural science and mathematics. The curriculum of higher education would further employ the "Seven Liberal Arts" and develop the reasoning powers through a study of the perennial ideas as found in "the great books." Ecclesiastical perennialists would include theological studies and all classical realists would emphasize philosophy, since as Hutchins states, ". . . the most practical education is the most theoretical one."

It is not the task of the true college or university to train for medicine, law, or teaching. Separate institutions should care for such vocational concerns, holds Hutchins. Likewise, the genuine university will not offer courses that are primarily utilitarian or for the commercial benefit of business and industry. Eclecticism, pragmatism, and positivism with their accompanying implications for education would be omitted.

c. *The Teacher's Task*

A teacher who practices the educational principles of classical realism would play a secondary and mediating role. He would not be a wellspring of knowledge, the center of the educative process, transmitting the cultural heritage. Rather, he would be as St. Thomas Aquinas stated, like a physician attempting to heal his patient. The teacher would also be like Socrates in his concern for universal ideas, with his challenging questions and demand for clearness and reason. Such a teacher would himself be an example of actuality attained.

Classical realism, more than any other school of educational thought, stresses the place of "mental discipline" in the educative process. Aristotle has been credited by some interpreters as supplying the basis for this theory. Schoolmen of the late Middle Ages promoted it in order to defend the teaching of certain classical subjects in universities under challenge to become more utilitarian. The theory fits in perfectly with the other tenets of perennialism. Since the task of education is to actualize the learner's potential, and this requires

the development of his reasoning powers, the disciplining and strength-
ening of the mind is a major obligation. A curriculum based on the
ancient Trivium is the primary means available to the student in the
achievement of the goals of liberation, rationality, and actuality.

d. The Relationship to Society

Not only the American community, but the people of the entire
world are faced with eventual annihilation if Western society continues in its present course, hold most perennialists. Because of the
influence of Roscellinus and Abelard, men have increasingly tended
toward nominalism, materialism, and pragmatism. The modern climate
favoring scientism has especially contributed to the prospect of human
extinction. For centuries man's appreciation for the permanent moral
and intellectual values has been eroding and now lies in ruin.

The only hope of the world is to return, at least in practice, to that
previous and more stable type of society which existed prior to the
introduction of nominalism. Revived in the main by the acceptance
of the one, true philosophy, it would be characterized by justice and
righteousness, and more fundamentally, by its pattern of permanent
truth in the midst of a changing modern world of particulars. Universal
concepts would be prior to all else, physical science would assume its
proper and subordinate relationship, and men would learn to distinguish fact from mere opinion.

Properly educated leadership must be available and in power
in order to achieve this new and philosophically-oriented society, and
thus avert world disaster. Classical realism offers the only kind of
education capable of preparing qualified leadership. The universities
would be required to perform the supreme task of creating an intel-
ectually elite class of leaders, schooled in philosophy, logical in
thought, and dedicated to achieving true values in themselves and in
society. These "philosopher-kings," to quote from Plato, would reform
society and, hopefully, by wise administration based on established
truth, bring about the good life for all men. Although the universities
would hold the paramount place, the church would need to assume
considerable responsibility in the creation of the new society, add
he ecclesiastical perennialists. The Unmoved Mover, God, the source

of all truth, would be recognized as superior to all else in the great
universal hierarchy.

C. EVALUATION AND CRITICISM

The strengths of perennialism have been noted as the school
was described in preceding pages. It is necessary here only to state
its most attractive aspect: It offers a permanent and stable program
both for society at large and the schools in particular. In such a
rapidly changing era, men need something unchanging to hold on to
in order to maintain a proper perspective. As for the schools, they can
never keep up with the changes in their society anyway. What the
schools need is a structure which requires no revision. Perennialism
offers this unchanging system of education.

We turn now to a consideration of the charges against and weak
nesses of classical realism.

1. Perennialism is founded upon "first principles" of philosophy
which are presumably the products of clear and rational thought
These truths perennialists hold to be obvious or self-evident to the
trained intellect. However, one is prompted to inquire why such
obvious facts are not evident to many more intelligent people and
to ask for an explanation for the volume of opposition from other
intellectual circles. Is it possible that the principles of perennialism
are also the opinions of mere men?

2. Classical realism's concept of truth provides a questionable
basis for teaching and learning. When truth is described as a universal
it implies that it is something "once and for all delivered to the saints."
It has long since been catalogued and deposited like gold in Heaven's
vault. In practice truth appears to have an element of change and to
be an active quality in whose creation man must participate.

3. Proponents of this school of educational thought favor the
selection of an elite group of intellectuals who would be educated
by the universities for leadership. Considerable power would be
vested in the hands of the few who would direct society, the uni
versities, the church, and the government. Although perennialists
assert that they are democratically-minded, does not their program
provide freedom for the new and acquiescence for the majority? Is
this democratic?

4. Classical realism offers an educational structure which presumably never needs any alteration. Would not the effect of such a program be to develop human personalities too ready to submit and too slow to challenge and object? Would not human initiative suffer in such a situation?

5. The theory of mental discipline has been the frequent target of modern psychology. Its basic premise was the assumption that the human brain was like a muscle and the strength of one segment could be utilized by adjacent or near segments, thus making for a high degree of transfer of learning. Modern psychologists hold that in no way is the mind like a muscle. Furthermore, transfer of training is based not on the adjacency of segments of the brain but rather on the degree of similarity between the two or more learning situations.

6. Classical realism directs the attention of educators to the mind and intellect of the learner. This is in harmony with the philosophical position of the supremacy of universals. Yet it appears to most modern educators that certain pupil and accidental particulars such as the health of the physical body and the student's total material environment are also important factors in the learning process. Is not, then, the perennialist restriction an undesirable one?

7. Neo-Thomism has found expression in the programs of education in parochial schools. And the administrators, especially the supervising clergy, are particularly critical of the goals of universal public education. Is there not a degree of inconsistency here in that while criticizing the society which gives them the freedom to operate separate schools, they are meanwhile most eager to obtain funds from that society to support their parochial program?

8. The term "classical" implies a reference to something that transpired many centuries ago. Where once a classical education was the only acceptable kind, today in a different age, it seems extremely irrelevant. The Western World is science-minded, pragmatic, and liberal in a new sense. Modern man is proud of what he is and does not intend to regress to absolutism.

FURTHER READING

Brameld, Theodore. *Patterns of Educational Philosophy.* New York: World Book Company, 1950.

Brameld, Theodore. *Philosophies of Education in Cultural Perspective*. New York: The Dryden Press, Inc., 1955.

Broudy, Harry S. *Building a Philosophy of Education* (2nd ed.). Englewood Cliffs, New Jersey: Prentice-Hall, Inc., 1961.

Gordon, John R. "Classicism, Pragmatism, and Essentialism," *Educational Quest*, Vol. XIII, No. 1 (Winter, 1969), pp. 3-10.

Hutchins, Robert Maynard. *The Conflict in Education*. New York: Harper Brothers, 1953.

Hutchins, Robert Maynard. *The Learning Society*. New York: F. A. Praeger Publisher, 1968.

Hutchins, Robert Maynard. *Some Observations on American Education*. Cambridge, Massachusetts: Cambridge University Press, 1956.

Keets, John. *Schools Without Scholars*. Boston: Houghton-Mifflin Co., 1958.

Kneller, George F. *Foundations of Education*. New York: John Wiley and Sons, Inc., 1963.

Newman, John Henry Cardinal. *The Idea of a University*. London: Longmans, Green and Company, 1886

Phenix, Philip H. (ed.). *Philosophies of Education*. New York: John Wiley and Sons, Inc., 1961.

Van Doren, Mark. *Liberal Education*. Boston: Beacon Press, 1959.

Wingo, G. Max. *The Philosophy of American Education*. New York: Heath and Company, 1965.

"The Classical Realist Approach to Education," a film. New Film Service, Indiana University, Bloomington, Indiana.

Chapter VI

RECONSTRUCTIONISM,
The Sociological Solution

The complete title of this school of thought is social reconstructionism. Its views proceed from a concern for contemporary and
future world society, and its basis is the behavioral sciences, instead
of religion, Greek thought, and the experience of the individual,
which characterize other schools of educational theory. Although
there appears to be a high degree of similarity to progressivism, of
which this theory is now a well-developed extension, social reconstructionism differs significantly in emphasis and practice. An appreciation for its position requires an understanding of its development in the United States.

A. HISTORICAL BACKGROUND

Subsequent to the economic collapse in 1929, progressivism began
to alter its course. A significant number of American educators of note
moved from the emphasis on individual interests and child-centeredness to a concern for the community as a whole. The earliest writers
to give evidence of this trend were progressivists. Both John Dewey
in "My Pedagogic Creed," and elsewhere, and his former student,
William Heard Kilpatrick, expressed a genuine interest in the relationship of the American school to society and held that social reconstruction was a task of our educational institutions. Dewey unwittingly
suggested a name for the new school of thought with the publication
in 1920 of his well-known book entitled, *Reconstruction in Philosophy*.
The economic and political problems of the 1930's added impetus to

the movement as did the shift during the same period in federal government policy from a laissez-faire attitude toward social needs to a marked concern for the general welfare. It is certain that the rise during this period in history of certain totalitarian regimes also had an effect on social and educational theory in the United States.

The development of social reconstructionism during its early years was centered around a Columbia University professor named George S. Counts, one-time president of the American Federation of Teachers. His book, *The American Road to Culture,* appeared in 1930 and was followed two years later by a writing with a title which at the time seemed very radical. It was *Dare the Schools Build a New Social Order?* During the early 1930's the number of supporters of Counts' direct approach to social problems increased. One was Dr. John L. Childs who contributed a number of articles to the group's periodical, *The Social Frontier,* of which Counts was editor until 1937. Boyd H. Bode also should be named as an early social reconstructionist. However, Bode favored a more indirect approach to the solution of social problems than did the aforementioned educators. His position was expressed in a running debate in the periodical of the school of thought. The advocates of social reconstructionism were sometimes referred to by their opponents as "frontier thinkers" and criticized for holding membership in the American Federation of Teachers. Some concern was generated over the political aspirations of what was feared would be a "pedagogic party" with the headquarters at Columbia University in New York City.

Plans made near the end of the economic depression on the part of the social reconstructionists to work with organized labor for social improvements failed to materialize. The early leaders such as Counts and Bode lost the inertia necessary for reform as the country successfully struggled out of the great depression. But a new and vigorous leader had appeared on the scene by this time. Dr. Theodore Brameld, most recently of Boston University, was well-qualified in philosophy, political science, and academic education. He maintained that the proposition made by Counts in 1932 was still valid in spite of the changes and improvements in the country since that earlier day. Brameld first contributed articles to *The Social Frontier* beginning in 1934. Later in 1950, he published his *Patterns of Educational Philosophy* in which he set forth his blueprint for perfecting the American democracy by utilizing the system of public education. He has continued the struggle as evidenced by his now numerous articles and books dealing with the urgent need for a thorough reconstruction of the present social pattern. Brameld warns that the weight of unsolved problems could destroy the present culture altogether.

B. PHILOSOPHICAL FOUNDATIONS OF SOCIAL RECONSTRUCTIONISM

The body of thought which comprises the principles of social reconstructionism has long since attained the stature of a separate school of educational theory. Its roots, however, first found nurture among progressivists so that it, too, is related more to pragmatism than to any other school of general philosophy. Although that relationship is further removed from pragmatism than is that of its predecessor, the same affinity for the scientific approach has earned its supporters the title of neo-experimentalists. The sociological basis of the school will be noted in its position with regard to the major fields of general philosophy.

1. *Concept of Reality*

Social reconstructionism, unlike classical philosophies, rejects the concept of universals as a fundamental consideration. Reality to the social reconstructionist has to do with the aggregate of circumstances and conditions which surround and affect man's existence. Like progressivism, this philosophy emphasizes the primacy of human experiences but deals entirely with those that are group instead of individual. The view is that of "cultural reality," and under that title would be such social phenomena as the conflicts and agreements of groups in society, their loyalties, commitments, ideals, and relationships to others, as well as the historical development of the total community.

2. *Concept of Epistemology*

Social reconstructionism differs from progressivism in regard to knowledge and truth in that it is the goal-seeking society, not the individual, which is the beginning point. Generally, knowledge is generated by groups who question the goals of society and the methods employed to attain them. Mentioned as necessary factors are prehension which is viewed as an awareness of human needs, and apprehension which involves an understanding of parts and relationships. Reflective thinking should be employed as a method and is subordinate only to social consensus. This last, social consensus, requires (a) evidence of a desirable social goal, (b) communication with the community, (c) agreement on approaches, and (d) testing of the planned action in the society.

Truth has been determined when there is agreement as to the primary goals of the society and the methods to be employed to solve the problems necessary to attainment. To the social reconstructionist, truth involves the use of the "group mind," social agreement, logic, experimentation, and testing. True knowledge is always related to the society in the process of seeking agreed goals.

3. Concept of Axiology

Values are not ideas which are forever fixed somewhere. Rather, values are the goals of society as determined by social consensus. The social reconstructionist adds that even values so agreed upon may change as society changes, so that there are never any irrevocable values. Inevitably, values are related to cultural realities and include such human wants as sufficient food, proper protection from the elements, satisfaction, participation, educational opportunity, and many others. The supreme and all-inclusive value is social self-realization, which means the greatest possible degree of satisfaction of the individuals and groups of the society.

4. Social and Political Philosophy

No other philosophy has been as sociologically-minded as this one and none have proposed such a total reconstruction of the culture. The major proposals of its contemporary leaders can be reduced to specific areas as follows:

a. *Political*

An international government, democratic in policy, and committed to the carrying out of agreements reached by social consensus; improving conditions for all people everywhere; increasing communications between countries; assisting in the development of emerging nations.

A national government with the control of the economic structure, services, and utilities in the hands of the majority but with adequate representation of every segment and interest in the community; respect for minorities with guarantees of security and equal opportunity; an acceptance of the function of constructive criticism by minority groups; all decisions based not only on number of affirmative votes but on the basis of the fundamental principle of social self-realization.

b. *The Sciences*

Physical sciences utilized to serve the material needs of man; social sciences employed to make better communities, country and world; research in all the sciences to be encouraged by governmental leaders well-versed in sociology.

c. *Human Needs*

An economy that will provide full employment, minimum income, and sufficient means for all citizens; aid to the handicapped, companionship for the elderly, and security and social satisfaction for all.

C. EDUCATIONAL THEORY AND PRACTICE

The primary means for bringing about a reconstructed society would be an educational system supported in the main by the Federal Government. Instruction should be free and universal, and reach from the nursery school through the university. Education for adults, aesthetic advantages, freedom of expression, and creativity would characterize the educational program.

The educational aims of the reconstructionists cannot be separated from their social and political philosophy. Since those principles have already been named, it is necessary only to present the proposed changes in the practical operation of public education. The following information was extracted from the only source available, namely, the writings of Dr. Theodore Brameld.[1]

1. *Administration of the Schools*

Members of both state and local boards of control serving public education from kindergarten through university should be elected by the people. Their task should be to develop policies of education that would serve all segments of society and not certain subgroups as is often the case under current practices. Attached to each individual school there should be a number of advisory councils, one for each group of people involved, such as citizens, teachers, administrators, students, parents, other employees, and an all-school council whose members would be elected representatives from the above-named groups. Together these boards and councils would practice social consensus, impose agreed rules of conduct upon the pupils, and seek to improve the quality of learning. One other major assignment, formerly left to boards of education, would be for the councils at their respective levels to collectively elect those administrators who would execute their policies, including leaders in both public schools and in higher education.

2. *Organization of the Learning Program*

Theodore Brameld would alter the grade structure in the schools so as to conform to the following diagram:

School	Ages	Emphasis
Nursery	2-5	Guidance and Personal Development
Lower Elementary	6-11	Social Development and Related Qualities of Personality
Upper Elementary	12-16	Activities and Learning Preparatory to Secondary School

---

1. *Towards a Reconstructed Philosophy of Education* (New York: The Dryden Press, Inc., 1956).

School	Ages	Emphasis
Secondary	17-21	Equivalent to Present Junior and Senior Years of High School and First Two Years of College

It would be mandatory that all youths attend the aforementioned schools, although children less than three and one-half years of age may be excused if their mothers do not work outside the home. The school year would extend from January through December with two one-month vacation periods, one in the winter and one in the summer, and two one-week vacations, one in the spring and the other in the fall. Brameld would also keep the facilities of the school available to the community for adult education, counseling of all kinds, and supervised recreational activities. The schools would be open evenings, Saturdays, Sundays, and during vacation periods.

Although Brameld's recommendations are primarily directed toward the secondary school, there are directives for other levels as well. Pre-secondary pupils would acquaint themselves with fundamental skills and subject-emphasis, which in turn would prepare them for the advanced studies of the school next above them. Higher education would concern itself with teaching and research, especially in the behavioral and social sciences.

The secondary school would schedule its learning activities from 8:30 A.M. to 4:00 P.M., a seven and one-half hour day. Its program has been explained by reference to the parts of a carriage. The four wheels represent the four somewhat different years of education in the secondary school. The hub of each wheel represents the central theme of one year of work. This theme must always deal with some real problems in terms of the goals and wishes of society. Some examples are motivation and orientation to the secondary school program, the place of art and science, human relations, and the attainment of goals. These would draw upon community resources and knowledgeable persons for information. The supporting spokes of each wheel represent the emphasis on the use of discussion groups as well as the required courses and skills which characterize our high schools and colleges today. The rim suggests that the total program is unified and related to the central theme of the year's work.

Beyond Brameld's secondary school there would be institutions that offer education for admission to the professions, such as law, medicine, and teaching. Here, too, the students must learn to appreciate their obligations and responsibilities to their community. The entire structure of higher education should concern itself with the relationships between the multiple aspects of our evolving great society and work toward the supreme goal of social self-realization.

D. EVALUATION AND CRITICISM

Objections to social reconstructionism have come from two major sources. Academicians, including those who value the intellectual benfits derived from a profound study of classical literature, constitute one center of opposition. The other source has included those true experimentalists in education who resent any diluting or alteration of the original principles of progressivism. Following are some of the negative comments which have been directed toward this school of thought:

1. Social reconstruction is unrealistic. It offers a program which people are obviously unwilling to adopt and makes promises for a utopian future that most probably will never materialize. American or world society will never undergo the total reconstruction required by this theory.

2. There are some rather formidable factors which prevent the general acceptance of this school of thought. It would appear that social reconstructionists have underestimated the strength of our present political structure, the fact that human nature reacts negatively to such wholesale change, and the retarding effect of social inertia. Added to the above should be the power of vested interests and the real fear of socialism to which, some critics say, this program would lead.

3. This school of thought is self-contradictory. Social reconstructionism professes to be democratic in nature and even promotes the so-called method of "social consensus." At the same time society by social consensus is rejecting the theory which social reconstruction expounds. To continue to press its demands upon the government, educators, and society when its position has already been rejected is

not in keeping with the method of social consensus which is advanced by social reconstructionism.

4. The adoption of social reconstructionism as a working philosophy of education would be detrimental to some areas of scholarly and of social interest. Not only would there be less class time for strictly academic studies, but the resultant lack of sufficiently skilled manpower in our communities would handicap the development of the very society the reconstructionists propose to improve.

5. The chief task of the school is the education of the citizenry. It is not social reform. Educators must transmit the culture; that is historic and primary. Social improvement is only a segment of the larger task, and it must not be allowed to dominate the process of learning. Besides, the best way to make a better society is to help the individual but not through broad social programs, which, in their efforts to reach everybody, reach very few at all. In fact, such programs could damage society by reducing parental responsibility, personal initiative, and the value of the home as the basic social unit.

6. Social reconstructionism is not a philosophy of education. Rather, it is a sociology. Its theory has little connection with generally accepted philosophic bases and is therefore without an ultimate foundation. Even its support from the behavioral sciences is inexact and open to contradictory interpretations. It appears to have no reliable basis for its tenets.

FURTHER READING

Brameld, Theodore. *Cultural Foundations of Education.* New York: Harper and Brothers, 1957.

Brameld, Theodore. *Education as Power.* New York: Holt, Rinehart and Winston, 1965.

Brameld, Theodore. *Education for the Emerging Age.* New York: Harper and Row, 1965.

Brameld, Theodore. *Ends and Means in Education.* New York: Harper and Row, 1950.

Brameld, Theodore. *Patterns of Educational Philosophy.* New York: World Book Company, 1950.

Brameld, Theodore. *The Remaking of a Culture.* New York: Harper and Brothers, 1959.

Brameld, Theodore. *Towards a Reconstructed Philosophy of Education.* New York: The Dryden Press, Inc., 1965.

Counts, George S. *The American Road to Culture.* New York: The John Day Company, 1930.
Counts, George S. *Dare the Schools Build a New Social Order?* New York: The John Day Company, 1932.
Counts, George S. *Education and American Civilization.* New York: Teachers College, Columbia University, 1952.
Kneller, George F. *Foundations of Education.* New York: John Wiley and Sons, Inc., 1963.
Stanley, William O. *Education and Social Integration.* New York: Teachers College, Columbia University, 1953.
Wynne, John P. *Theories of Education.* New York: Harper and Row, 1963.

"A Reconstructionist View of Education," a film. New Film Service, Indiana University, Bloomington, Indiana.

Chapter VII

ANALYTIC PHILOSOPHY,
The Positive Position

Philosophy for at least the past century has evidenced an increasingly discernible trend away from the classical modes of thought. In the Western hemisphere especially, many thinkers have moved from abstract idealism to the utilitarian and empirical emphases, and thence to an acceptance of the methods employed by the exact sciences. Early in the present century there developed certain clusters of men and ideas which we may now consider as developmental of the movement broadly termed, analyticism. Generally, the proponents of its various branches agree on the unproductiveness of speculative metaphysics and insist that philosophy must offer clarification and positive information. The approach of this new mode of thought is primarily epistemological in a new sense combined with methods which are as objective as possible.

A. THE HISTORICAL DEVELOPMENT OF ANALYTICISM

1. *The Pythagoreans*

Most, if not all, philosophies can be traced back to propositions made in ancient time. In the case of positivism, the earliest efforts for which there are any records were made in the sixth century, B.C., by the Pythagoreans. This society of philosophers conducted scientific research into mathematics. While the Milesian theorists turned to physics in their efforts to understand the universe, the Pythagoreans interpreted everything in terms of geometry. Using the analogy of the seven-stringed lyre, specific numbers were assigned to every aspect which came to their attention, including physical health, morals, and sounds in music. The Pythagoreans held to the notion that precise numbers were the prior consideration and through the science of mathematics the harmony of the universe might be explained. Criticism of the Pythagorean tendency toward mystery religion eventually made them unpopular and combined with other forces to bring an end to their attempts to construct a positive metaphysics.

2. René Descartes

Except for some contributions from such men as Parmenides (b. 510 B.C.), philosophy had to await the coming of the great Frenchman, René Descartes (1596-1650) to develop further the relationship of mathematics to abstract theory. Descartes was a master in both fields and was, therefore, uniquely qualified to make his contribution. He held mathematics to be the exact science which alone could lead man to positive knowledge. Although Descartes may be properly referred to as a metaphysician, he did note the possibility of exchanging that field for mathematics as the basis for philosophical systems.

3. Baron Gottfried Wilhelm von Leibnitz

The noted German thinker, Leibnitz, was born just four years before Descartes' life came to an end. His dates (1646-1716) overlap, in turn, with those of John Locke who was an early empiricist. Leibnitz, like Descartes, was both a philosopher and a mathematician and was interested in synthesizing these two fields of study. He is noted here mainly because of his oft-expressed hope that metaphysicians someday would be equipped to determine their truths by the use of calculus.

4. Auguste Comte

Thus far, the historical development presented here has linked philosophy with mathematics; we now can relate philosophy to the physical sciences. Auguste Comte (1798-1857), a French thinker, agreed with many of the concepts promoted by the then rising British Utilitarians. Like them, he viewed science as a means of improving man's environment. His contribution, if it may be summarized quickly, was simply that he further developed the concept of philosophy as a more precise field of study by synthesizing aspects of it with the positive sciences. Comte saw this view as a possible solution to the many social problems which grew out of the Industrial Revolution. For his work he has been named "the founder of positive philosophy."

5. The Cambridge Group—George E. Moore and Bertrand Russell

The two philosophers most closely associated with the early development of this new movement in England met as students at Trinity College, Cambridge University. Bertrand Russell (1872-1970) had been there two years when George Edward Moore (1873-1958) arrived in 1892 and began his study of the classics. Russell diverted him to philosophy, and together they exerted tremendous influence against the extreme idealism of the Neo-Hegelian philosophers of which Francis Herbert Bradley (1846-1924) was during much of his life the best-known disciple. For many years Russell and Moore carried on a running debate concerning which one had influenced the other the most, and each insisting altruistically that he himself was the pupil and the other the teacher. Judging from the effects of Moore's publication in 1903, "Refutation of Idealism in Mind"[1] Russell may have been right, at least initially. Moore's work precipitated the new realist movement in England out of which a branch of analytic philosophy has grown. His procedure involved a painstaking delineation of each aspect of a proposition. The touchstone of truth is common sense, Moore held. And a common sense belief is one which is universally acknowledged by everyone, including philosophers, to be true. This view of the world and concern for ordinary language was quite the opposite of the abstract idealism which had occupied the minds of most English philosophers. In writing his famous *Principia Ethica*

---

1. *Philosophical Studies* (London: Kegan Paul, 1921).

(1903) Moore continued to employ the measure of common sense. His contributions, however, did not earn him a place among the logical atomists.

The life and works of Betrand Russell, the most controversial philosopher of modern time, constitute an impressive chronicle. His godfather was the British Utilitarian, John Stuart Mill, and his grand-father, Lord John Russell, was once Prime Minister of England. Bereft of his parents at an early age, he was raised by Christian relatives. Against their wishes he became interested in philosophy and by the time he was eighteen years of age, he had rejected their puritan religion and, like his father, became an atheist. He loved the academic life of Trinity College, Cambridge University, where he was first a brilliant student and later a professor. Since then, Russell lectured extensively in the United States but not without objections. In 1940 he was appointed professor of philosophy at the College of the City of New York which assignment aroused the fury of certain citizens. Called "bigots" by others, they denounced the appointment as "The establishment of a chair of indecency." Because of Russell's previously published views on marriage and morals, he was declared a threat to the ethics of the youth. After a trial, the appointment was withdrawn.

Russell studied mathematics during his first three years at Cambridge and then turned to philosophy. He first became enamored with Hegelianism and the ideas of F. H. Bradley, but by 1898 both he and his friend, G. E. Moore, had abandoned idealism for a more positive view. Eventually differences in the philosophy of Moore and Russell became evident. Moore with a classical background viewed philosophy as a process of analysis based on ordinary language and common sense, while Russell led the way toward a logical analysis, a procedure much like those of the exact sciences and requiring a precise vocabulary. Of note at this point is the publication of the treatise, *Principia Mathematica* (1910-1913) by Russell and Alfred North Whitehead (1861-1947), which reduces mathematics to logic and prescribes a perfect, logical language. In summary, the perplexities of philosophy were to be solved not by the use of speculative metaphysics but by use of a system of logic employing algebraic-like symbols.

It must not be assumed from the foregoing that Russell and Whitehead remained in the same school of thought. Both men were mathematicians, but Russell employed his early training to further the development of an objective philosophy, which became known specifically as logical atomism. Whitehead, on the other hand, tended toward Platonism and classicism. He eventually resigned his professorship in mathematics and spent the last years of his life lecturing in classical philosophy at Harvard University.

6. *Ludwig Wittgenstein*

Russell's most famous pupil was Austrian-born Ludwig Wittgenstein (1889-1951) whose first interest was not philosophy at all. He studied architecture in Germany and England, and then in 1911 became a student under Russell at Cambridge, eventually exerting more influence over his teacher than Russell did over him. Before the First World War, Wittgenstein returned to Austria. Somehow, while participating in the war he was able to write the *Tractatus Logico-Philosophicus,* which appeared in German in 1921 and in English a year later.[2] For approximately ten years thereafter Wittgenstein abandoned philosophy, feeling that he had said the final word and there was nothing more to add. When his interest in philosophy was revived in 1929, he returned to Cambridge where he became a regular member of the faculty. From 1929 until 1947 Wittgenstein occupied the chair of philosophy at Cambridge previously filled by G. E. Moore. It might be added that a pupil of Wittgenstein, John Wisdom (1904-   ), another analyticist, followed his master to this same position. After John Wisdom's retirement, an important epoch concluded at Cambridge and positivism, or analyticism, took on a new character in a new place, Oxford University.

The work of Wittgenstein is commonly divided into so-called early and later periods with the *Tractatus* the basis for the first and his *Philosophical Investigations,* published posthumously in 1953, the source of information for the latter period. In the earlier writing Wittgenstein viewed the natural sciences as a source of true propositions with a distinctive task, that of finding new facts. Philosophy,

---

2. New York: Harcourt Brace and Company.

on the other hand, should not attempt to discover new truths but should be an activity which would solve puzzles, elucidate, and clarify ideas obtained from other sources. The philosophers have been mistaken as to the logic of our langauge, he held, and the result has not been truth or falsity but meaningless nonsense. A true proposition, such as one from the natural sciences, is a faithful portrayal of reality. It is an "atomic proposition," a picture which reveals the particular structure and arrangement of objects and facts. The philosopher should not philosophize as to the truth of scientific data, but he should criticize the language and formulate statements concerning it. In effect, this role makes it impossible for the philosopher to propose any concepts in the fields of religion and ethics since these are beyond both the scope of the natural sciences and philosophy. In sum, the *Tractatus* outlines the limits of language, treats its structure and indicates what philosophers should not try to say. Eventually Wittgenstein admitted that some of his own propositions were nonsensical, but nevertheless, relevant and significant nonsense.

Ten years after completing the *Tractatus*, Wittgenstein altered his position and repudiated much of what he had said previously. Apparently all the problems of philosophy had not been solved. His concern thereafter as expressed in his *Philosophical Investigations* is with words which may be used like tools in "language games." We employ words to express a great variety of functions. Words have many uses and there is no one way by which words obtain definition. Meaning is derived from use and based on rules which we must observe. Every philosopher, thinker, and speaker uses words with meanings contingent upon the particular context in which he places them. This, to some degree, makes meaning relative. The philosopher's task now is to describe language as it is; it is not to write a new and precise one by the use of symbols. He should study the rules of the innumerable language games, and then strive for linguistic clearness. The *Tractatus* and the *Philosophical Investigations* both hold that philosophy should not indulge in metaphysical speculation; that philosophy is primarily an activity which deals with language. The two works differ in their concepts of language and in the way in which language should be analyzed. The early work is rigid in definition as compared to the complex and flexible approach accepted by the latter. In place of subscribing to Russell's logical atomism, Wittgenstein in his later period promotes philosophy as a method of studying the countless uses of language in order to solve philosophical perplexities. In effect, he moved from the study of logic and the perfect language to a study of the ordinary functions of language.

7. The Vienna Circle

The appointment in 1922 of Moritz Schlick, noted as an interpreter of Einstein, to a professorship in the philosophy of science at the University of Vienna, provided the leadership for a new group of like-minded scholars on that campus. Schlick, strongly negative to metaphysics himself, drew about him a select group of scientists and mathematicians. Included were such future spokesmen as Rudolph Carnap who came to Vienna in 1926 and Friedrick Waismann, both of whom later became lecturers in American and British universities, respectively. The group readily accepted the *Tractatus* as a major focus of study, but there was only a very informal relationship with its author who never joined with his Viennese supporters. The professors at the University of Vienna who were involved first began with seminars and discussions and then quickly formalized their organization. The name by which history remembers the group appeared first in 1929 with the publication of "The Scientific Outlook of the Vienna Circle." Its members were already known as logical positivists or logical empiricists. For most of its history the group operated with no professional contact with the English movement and in time some members even became critical of their counterparts at Cambridge. In 1929 the Vienna Circle held an international congress in Prague. Other conferences followed in Copenhagen, Paris, and even Cambridge. A regular journal was published and a series of pamphlets appeared before the organization began to disintegrate. There were a number of reasons for the demise of the Circle such as the deaths of several members, including that of the leader, Schlick, who in 1936 was shot by an emotionally overwrought student, and the opposition of the rising Nazi party. Differences arose in the late 1930's in connection with the defense of their doctrines, and a number of the logical positivists moved away, some to England, but most to the

United States making the latter country a new center for the Movement. Rudolph Carnap, for example, taught in philosophy at the University of California at Los Angeles from 1954 until his death in 1970.

The position of the Vienna Circle, based on its interpretation of Wittgenstein's *Tractatus*, was that philosophy is an activity which makes for logical clarification of concepts. It serves to fix limits on language, to separate sense from nonsense, and to replace confusion with clarity. Philosophy does not so much solve problems as it dissolves them. Further, it should focus on means, not on ends as it does in the classical modes of thought, and on meaning, not on the nature of truth. Of great importance to the Vienna Circle was the now-famous principle of verifiability. Wittgenstein had said that there were three types of sentences: tautologies, such as definitions and contradictions which tell us nothing; meaningless statements such as are found in metaphysics and ethics; and significant sentences. The last presents truths that are verifiable by sense perception. Propositions which can be proven true by a direct or indirect appeal to the senses met the rquirements of Wittgenstein's principle. Such empirically meaningful statements are always synthetic, not analytic—which reminds one of Immanuel Kant's similar division of human judgments. An analytic statement is one in which the predicate logically restates what is already presented by the subject of the sentence. An example would be, "Fathers are males," which is an obvious a priori truth based on the terms employed and analyzed. On the other hand, "Fathers are workers" does not necessarily present a fact. Something not included in the proposition must be added to determine if the statement is true or false. This latter, the synthetic proposition, is the only meaningful kind of statement, since it can be verified empirically, that is, by sense experience.

At least two major emphases of Wittgenstein and his supporters in Vienna are greatly similar to views held by the American pragmatists. Both philosophies have something to do with the clarity of propositions and also attach major importance to empiricism. These points of similarity do not characterize all the supporters of logical positivism at any time in history. Note too, that although the Vienna Circle accepted the "early" Wittgenstein, it could not have been agreeable to the "later" Wittgenstein as revealed in his *Philosophical Investigations*.

B. PRESENT POSITION

Analytic philosophy has become the most prominent mode of thought among philosophers of the Western World. Its approach dominates and characterizes the professional activities of academicians as seen in their conventions, lectures and publications, including books and periodicals. This is true in regard to both general and educational philosophy. Following are concise statements on the present status of analyticism.

1. *Alfred Jules Ayer*

Logical positivism has been represented in England in recent years by Alfred Jules Ayer (1910-   ), once a pupil of Gilbert Ryle (1900-   ) and later of Schlick and Carnap in Vienna. Earlier in his career, Ayer became England's leading exponent of logical positivism, but later he so differed with the Viennese that he openly criticized his great teacher, Carnap. With the passing of the years, Ayer has modified his strict form of logical positivism and become more subtle and flexible. His *Language Truth and Logic,* which first appeared in 1936, has become a first source of information for a newer branch of analyticism, language analysis. It might be added that in 1960 Ayer himself joined the faculty of Oxford University, England, as a professor of logic.

2. *Oxford University*

The most prominent center in England in the historical development of analyticism was most certainly Cambridge University. Some of the leaders there, as already mentioned, were Moore, Russell, and Wittgenstein. But when Professor John Wisdom (1904-   ) retired from the Cambridge faculty, this marked the end of a period. Meanwhile a number of younger professors at Oxford University had become concerned with logical positivism or logical empiricism. Led by Gilbert Ryle, noted for his studies of Wittgenstein and his work with "logical grammar," and by several other brilliant minds, Oxford University during the 1930's and 1940's became the new center of British analyticism, a distinction which it maintains at this writing.

3. Analyticism in the United States

As elsewhere in academic circles of the Western World, so in the United States analyticism is now the dominant philosophical movement. For detailed examples of this newer mode of philosophy as taught in American colleges and universities one should read *Ethics and Language* by Charles Leslie Stevenson (1908-   ). This professor from the University of Michigan at Ann Arbor was the first to develop the emotive theory of ethics showing how we use language more than logic in the process of persuasion. Another thinker of similar interests is Willard Van Quine (1908-   ), a prominent American philosopher from Harvard University and a former student at Oxford. In the field of educational philosophy the leading representative is Israel Scheffler (1923-   ) of Harvard University whose book, *Conditions of Knowledge* should be required reading for every would-be professional educator.

4. Major Branches

The major concern at this point is not with subtle distinctions, historical or contemporary, between the various positions held by different philosophers in the process of developing analyticism—that is the task of general philosophy. It is necessary, though, that the contributions from the major sources be associated with the two major branches of analyticism which currently exist, namely logical empiricism and linguistic analysis.

a. Logical Empiricism

Used somewhat interchangeably today are the terms logical empiricism, scientific empiricism, and logical positivism, the latter title coming from the Vienna Circle. An outline of the development of this branch would involve the contributions of Auguste Comte, Bertrand Russell and his logical atomism, the "early" Wittgenstein and his *Tractatus,* and the Vienna Circle including Carnap and Schlick. The supporters of logical empiricism, the historically developed title, have been characterized by varying degrees of adherence to Wittgenstein's principle of verification. It will be remembered that this principle required that a proposition be tested by the direct method, that is by sense perception, or by the indirect method which involves a series of logical deductions leading to a prediction which itself may then be tested empirically. Such verifiable synthetic propositions were regarded by previous logical empiricists as the only meaningful type of statement. More recent philosophers of this movement are inclined now to view statements having to do with ethics, aesthetics, and religion as having some importance in human life. One further characteristic of logical empiricism has been its concern for the development of an algebraic-like language in which symbols would represent precise terms and concepts. Bertrand Russell actually developed such a system as a means to the unification of all the sciences. It is recognized today that such a system is not possible. What is possible and necessary is clear, unemotive communication, unaffected by subjective factors, and utilizing terminology that is simplified, precise, and consistent. The way science uses mathematics to express its truths is an example of the type of approach we might hope for in philosophy.

b. *Linguistic Analysis*

The "ordinary language" philosophers can trace their development from the work of G. E. Moore, the "later" Wittgenstein and his *Philosophical Investigations,* to A. J. Ayer and the leadership of recent years at Oxford University, and to particular professors in the United States. This branch of philosophical analysis differs from the previously-mentioned one as follows: While logical empiricism has been concerned with developing a symbolic and precise language that would unify the sciences, linguistic analysis has sought to develop methods and criteria for use in analyzing language. This latter branch is concerned with the definitions of terms and meanings of propositions. Its proponents are interested in clarification through the use of paradigmatic approaches.

A commonly-used example is the distinction made by the linguistic analysists with regard to the words "use" and "usage." While many scholars see little need to be so precise, these ordinary language philosophers maintain that the word "use" refers to the correct use of language in terms of intended meaning, while "usage" indicates the way most people employ the language. Linguistic analysis seeks to both direct us toward greater precision in the use of language and also to separate those propositions which are capable of clear meanings from those which are not. It would appear that linguistic analysis has a wider scope of activity than logical empiricism and, also, has a greater potential effect on the field of professional and academic education.

5. *Principles of Analytic Philosophy*

The foregoing exposition of the development of analyticism, although admittedly concise, has already pointed out the important tenets of the movement. It is necessary now to state those doctrines in an organized fashion. Here, then, is a listing of principles or aspects of the general philosophy of analyticism, each one overlapping somewhat with every other one. In the order given they are the province, the method, the nature, and the goal of true philosophy.

a. The province of philosophy is not metaphysics, nor is it axiology; it is epistemology and logic. Attempts by philosophers to deal with metaphysical problems have been unproductive, involved an illegitimate use of language, and have yielded only nonsense and non-verifiable propositions. Likewise, axiological studies have provided no truths, but only preferences, and emotively-based personal values. Even the knowledge of God, if not denied altogther, is an experience which must be validated.

The various branches of analyticism have been united as to the province of philosophical activity. To limit the task to one field, the epistemological, is to restrict philosophy to a very narrow range indeed. Analyticism is, thus, concerned with types of statements, whether analytical or synthetic, and the evidences which guarantee the existence of truth.

b. The method of philosophy is analytical. Truth is not necessarily part of a system, and philosophy should not erect such structures. Philosophical propositions tell us nothing that can be proven. In brief, to philosophize is to analyze, not to speculate.

c. The nature of philosophy is objective. This means that it is closely related to the exact sciences and to mathematics and even entertains the possibility of developing a symbolic language, or at least one that is very firm and highly precise. On the negative side, analyticism is anti-subjective, anti-emotive, and anti-relative. It is not concerned with romantic and poetic literature. Normative propositions are not its business. Its interest is with the verified "isness" of a statement; not the "oughtness."

d. The goal of philosophy is clarification. It purposes to reveal truth and expose fallacy and nonsense by demanding exact meaning and developing precise definitions.

C. EDUCATION AND ANALYTICISM

The thoughtful reader may well wonder if a philosophy of education is possible under analyticism, given the limited province and restricted nature of the school. Obviously there would be no metaphysical position and no axiological one. The approach by this school to education, or for that matter, to any field of knowledge, would be by way of analytical epistemology.

Further, it is agreed that analyticism, as an important force in the general and social "climate of thought," has already brought about some change in the character of Western education. Some of the effects have been direct and others indirect, depending somewhat on whether the analyticists and educators involved view education as an art or a science, which itself is a very old controversy. The effects of logical empiricism have been evident indirectly, that is through those areas which are truly "foundational" to education, the behavioral sciences. The more direct and significant effects have come from the linguistic analysists who appear to view the field of education primarily as an art.

Analyticism is still a relatively new movement and sufficient time has not yet elapsed so that its effects on education can be easily discerned, let alone measured. Judging from the present character and direction of the movement, we can state with some certainty the position of analyticism with regard to each of the following areas:

1. *Foundations of Education*

The term "foundations," when used in relation to the field of professional education, refers to those basic assumptions, principles, and sometimes to scientific data, which give both reason and basis for what educators do in practice. These directives for teachers, counselors, administrators, and others in the field are drawn from specific academic areas, namely, philosophy of education, history of education, psychology of education, and sociology of education. The last-named area includes politics, economics, and anthropology as related to the field of education, and there are other subgroups as well. The point here is simply that given the nature of analyticism and the content of the foundations of education, the amount of acceptable subject matter in the latter would be greatly reduced. Analyticism is interested only in verifiable, synthetic propositions and not in value statements and other philosophical propositions.

There might well be no philosophy of education at all; only the inclination to define, analyze, and clarify the vocabulary involved. History of education would yield direction to educators only after the events named were proven factual and the results verified by experts. Psychology and sociology of education would probably fare somewhat better, since at least some of the guidance offered to educators by the behavioral sciences is a few degrees more precise than that which comes from the humanities.

2. *Role of the Teacher*

The amount of subject matter content acceptable for transmission would be reduced. As a result the teacher would probably do less lecturing but a great deal of critical thinking. In fact, he would need to be prepared by his years in college to be analytical and to become an example in logical thought for his students to follow. As an authority in modern epistemology he would set up precise rules for class discussion; he would demand clear definitions, and objective proof for every statement purported to be true. Abstractions would not be admitted, and every effort would be made to reduce the effects of human emotion on learning. The relationship of teacher to pupil would be instrumental and precise as compared to the more diffuse approach of the psychologically-oriented classroom.

3. Role of the Pupil

Academic freedom as a principal of operation would assume greater importance. The pupil would have both obligation and right to demand proven truths and established facts. His own feelings like those of the instructor would not enter in. Cooperation in the never-ending search for provable propositions would provide pupil and teacher with a common goal. The demand for freedom would be academic, not personal, and result in the development of a logical mind capable of restating a proven truth by a proper sequence of thought.

4. Subject Matter

The inclination of a learning situation committed primarily to analytic philosophy would be to emphasize the place of logic, mathematics, and the exact sciences. Arts, both liberal and fine, would have less to offer, while classical philosophy and religion might well have no place at all.

In all probability language studies would be important in such a school. Linguistic analysis would be basic to the discovery and validation of truth in all other fields of study.

5. Methods of Teaching

Analyticism, if adopted as a philosophy of education, would give rise to what might be termed the objectivity-centered classroom. The approach to learning would always be through real and carefully defined problems and employ methods which are as empirical as possible. Extensive use would be made of machine teaching and programmed learning in order to make the content purely objective.

6. *Relationship to Society*

Analyticism has proposed no program for societal improvement, so important in any modern theory of education. Indirectly, however, this new movement might make a most important contribution. Many of the present social problems and their proposed solutions need to be carefully analyzed for truth. Government programs in particular need to be studied critically and verified before further funds are appropriated. There could, thus, be several very tangible benefits to the society at large stemming from this new mode of thought.

D. EVALUATION AND CRITICISM

1. A comparison of the content of analytical philosophy with that of the orthodox schools of thought raises the question, "Is analyticism even a philosophy?" Thus far the only field in which it has offered us any truths is that of epistemology. Analyticism does not treat axiology since value propositions are only emotively-based preferences. It cannot deal with metaphysics, and offer us any "first" principle, because such statements cannot be verified empirically. Even if recent trends in analyticism seem to include a moderate degree of well-tempered metaphysics, the range of philosophy remains greatly reduced. It might be only a philosophy of science which relegates classical thought to an extremely subordinate position.

If analyticism is a philosophy, it is, even then, not a system of thought. Perhaps it may be called a school, or better, simply a movement.

2. If analyticism is not a philosophy, and educational theory requires such a foundation, then it may be that there is no possible connection between this movement and education. To state it another way: does not analyticism make educational philosophy impossible? If both metaphysics and axiology are ruled out of the foundation in general philosophy, then there is insufficient support for a philosophy of education. And a philosophy of education without a value theory is no philosophy at all. The limited offerings of analyticism make for a limited application to life and education. Always, the practical requires a base in the theoretical.

3. Analyticism has been criticized for its use of a single approach to truth. It is, as its name states, analytical. Philosophers through the centuries have employed this method but never to the exclusion of all others. Mature thinkers have long recognized that the nature of the material under study determines the choice of the method to be employed. Analyticism, in part, is limited in method because it limits its area of study.

4. None of the proponents of the various branches of analyticism have deducted from their philosophy any implications for societal improvement. During that time in history when education was based upon Calvinistic theology, there was little value in educating the masses so as to improve their lot in life. One's position and circumstances were determined in advance and were not to be questioned or altered. Now, in a more enlightened day, public education demands a base that is social and philosophical, not religious. And any philosophy that offers no social implications has automatically restricted its value to the field of education.

5. The demand for pure objectivity has certain effects which are unacceptable to the current majority of people. With regard to religion, analyticism has no place for the concept of God, is not interested in any kind of theology, and gives no credence to faith and commitment. Further, pure objectivity to some degree negates human emotions, and dehumanizes every area of life it deems worthy of its attention. Finally, there is the charge that the insistence of positivism for logical and objective truth would tend to restrict the spontaneity and creativity of the learner. Such an effect would reduce the quality of education offered in the classroom and its practical advantages to life as a whole. Analyticism can teach us mathematics, science, and a kind of logic, but it may be that it cannot offer us an education in the true sense. For where there is no basic theory, there is no direction—which is the task of philosophy after all.

FURTHER READING

Brown, L. M. *General Philosophy in Education*. New York: McGraw-Hill Book Company, 1966.
Dupuis, Adrian M. *Philosophy of Education in Cultural Perspective*. Chicago: Rand McNally and Company, 1966.

Gilson, Etienne (gen. ed.). *Recent Philosophy*. New York: Random House, Inc., 1962.

Gowin, D. Bob. "The Structure of Knowledge," *Educational Theory*. Vol. XX, No. 4 (Fall, 1970), pp. 319-328.

Gross, Barry R. *Analytic Philosophy*. New York: Pegasus, 1970.

Hospers, John. *An Introduction to Philosophical Analysis*. New York: Prentice-Hall, Inc., 1953.

Kneller, George F. (ed.). *Foundations of Education*. New York: John Wiley and Sons, Inc., 1963.

Kneller, George F. *Logic and Language of Education*. New York: John Wiley and Sons, Inc., 1966.

Maloney, Cornelius L. *Logical Positivism and American Education*. A Dissertation Abstract. Washington, D. C.: The Catholic University of America Press, 1951.

Mays, Wolfe. "Linguistic Analysis and the Philosophy of Education," *Educational Theory*. Vol. 20, No. 3 (Summer, 1970), pp. 269-283.

McMahon, Michael B. "Positivism and the Public Schools," *Phi Delta Kappan*. Vol. LI, No. 10 (June, 1970), pp. 515-517.

Naess, Arne (trans.). *Four Modern Philosophers*. Chicago: The University of Chicago Press, 1969.

Newsome, George L., Jr. "Analytic Philosophy and Theory of Education," *Proceedings of the Sixteenth Annual Meeting of the Philosophy of Education Society*, published by the Society, June, 1960.

Passmore, John. *A Hundred Years of Philosophy*. New York: The Macmillan Company, 1957.

Scheffler, Israel. *Conditions of Knowledge*. Chicago: Scott, Foresman and Company, 1965.

Scheffler, Israel. *The Language of Education*. Springfield, Illinois: Charles C Thomas Company, 1960.

Scheffler, Israel. *Philosophy and Education*. Boston: Allyn and Bacon, Inc., 1958.

Smith, S. L. "The First-Order Analysis of 'Education,'" *Educational Theory*, Vol. 20, No. 4 (Fall, 1970), pp. 386-398.

Soltis, Jonas F. *An Introduction to the Analysis of Educational Concepts*. Reading, Massachusetts: Addison-Wesley Publishing Company, 1968.

Urmson, J. O. *Philosophical Analysis*. London: Oxford University Press, 1956.

Waismann, Friedrick. *The Principles of Linguistic Philosophy*. New York: St. Martin's Press, 1965.

Chapter VIII

EXISTENTIALISM,
The Encounter with Subjectivity

Existentialism is not the title of one particular school of philosophy. Rather, it is the name of a newer mode of thought which encom-
passes so many variations and opposing views that any single name
becomes almost misleading. The meaning of its title is so elusive that
while some regard it as synonymous with the bizarre, the evil, and the
vile, others see it as a vitalizing force for the Christian religion.

It is true that with this new approach, philosophy does move from
its limited focus of the college classroom and from inter-institutional
debate to the man-in-the-street. The tenets of existentialism are thus
closely related to all persons, the tutored and the untutored alike.

Existentialism has not provided a ready-made system of easy
answers, and since its base is comprised of individualism, personal
freedom and choice, and of the confused and unpredictable aspects
of human existence, existentialism will never be such a source. At this
stage in history it must be accepted as a definite movement which
permeates the field of philosophy, human thought, and action in
Western society in general, and with implications for educational
practice.

A. HISTORICAL DEVELOPMENT

Existentialism as a separate and distinguishable mode of thought
appeared about one century ago. Like analyticism it represented a
revolt against the prevailing climate of philosophic thought, but its
movement was in the diametrically opposite direction. While analyti-

cism protested the vague idealism of Hegel and advocated an approach
that was mathematical, scientific and objective, existentialism voiced
its disfavor of any tendency that would enslave and manipulate human
personality, and vowed to rediscover the individual, the inner man,
the subjective.

The French Revolution (1789-1799) may be considered part of
the social milieu which gave rise to existentialism. Then, in France,
and also at the same time in Germany, men were increasingly inveigh-
ing against a social system which kept them bound. They wanted
freedom from ignorance, from social controls imposed by those in
power, and from ecclesiarchs who used religion for subjugation. Some
brave men dared to wonder out loud if perhaps the voice of the
church was more like the voice of ambitious men than the voice of God.

1. Soren Kierkegaard (1813-1855)

Kierkegaard, a Danish theologian with extraordinary literary ability, was the first existentialist. He provided the new mode of thought
with a title and stated the early directives. In view of these significant
contributions he has received little acclaim, and even today, his work
is overshadowed by that of lesser men.

As a person he was small of stature, a hunchback, physically weak
and chronically ill. In addition he had severe psychological problems
due to the absence in childhood of his own parents and a secure home
and also from the knowledge of his father's infidelity. Alone, melan-
cholic, and extremely sensitive to his own feelings, he one time became
so despondent that he cursed God. Although he repented, his outburst
remained on his conscience for the rest of his life and only added
to his despair.

Kierkegaard's great opportunity for happiness came through his
love for a girl named Regina Olsen. She returned his affection and
marriage was proposed. Then, fearing that his morbid personality
would seriously inhibit her happiness, Kierkegaard voluntarily broke
off the relationship. He ever remembered the woman he loved, and
never married.

As for education, Kierkegaard early in life received schooling that
was highly academic, intellectual, and intensely religious, but which
apparently did not include studies in the natural sciences. He even

tually enrolled at the University of Copenhagen and there settled on a career in theology. Later, he directed his literary ability and genuine concern for the feelings of men to the writing of his first important work, *Either-Or*, which appeared in 1843. His publications made him financially independent for life, if not popular.

Any general commentary on Kierkegaard's writings would need to state that he was negative to institutionalized, faithless religion, especially that represented by the Danish State Church, and to classical philosophy with its systematic and logical structures. Rationalism, he held, leads to determinism and limits man. Kierkegaard opposed any and all forces which would tend to dehumanize the individual.

Like other existenialists, the beginning point for Kierkegaard's philosophy is the concept of existence. To him it was absurd to start with the essence of being, and by some logical sequence, proceed to an analysis and explanation of change and movement, as classical thinkers had been doing for centuries. Kierkegaard focused his thoughts on the personal and subjective existence of the individual and vigorously fought against the theoretical constructs that would submerge and depersonalize man. Although he objected to the church as he saw it, and was intensely anti-clerical, he remained staunchly theistic and desired only to bring about a revitalization of true Christianity by elevating the individual believer to his rightful place. This conversion of religion and a return to true faith was for Kierkegaard the only solution to the moral dilemma of society.

2. Friedrich Wilhelm Nietzsche (1844-1900)

A noted German thinker, Nietzsche began his philosophy with the statement, "God is dead!" His notion was that man has in effect done away with God and replaced Him with rationalism, scientism, and objectivity. And if God is dead, then the churches are dead, religion is of no value any longer, and man is most certainly alone with his predicament and his decisions. It is not difficult to see why Nietzsche is regarded as an early atheistic existentialist which contrasts sharply with the fervent theism of Kierkegaard. Nietzsche's objection to religion, rationalism, and objectivity, and in general, his nihilistic philosophy, does correspond favorably with existentialism's position that there are no universals and no fixed values. The only

hope for mankind is a subjectivist philosophy. Nietzsche also object
to equal opportunities for all on the ground that this principle lead
to unequal opportunities for those with exceptional potential and
unusual talent.

3. Early Existentialism in France and Germany

Modern existentialism appeared almost simultaneously but sep
arately in France and Germany during the early decades of thi
century. It is conceded that the social and political conditions in
Western Europe following World War I and World War II were
factors in the meteoric rise of this new mode of thought. The stresse
of working with the underground movements with the ever-presen
possibility of torture and death and of living under the occupation
desiring freedom and liberty, had much to do with this new climate
of thought.

a. The most noted of early French existentialists is Gabrie
Marcel (1889-   ). Of Jewish background, he was first a Protestan
and then a Roman Catholic. His writings are not only completely
theistic; they defend the great synthesis of Thomas Aquinas and view
true religion and personal faith in God as indispensable factors in
man's quest for an understanding of personal existence.

Also involved in this quest is the aspect of direct communication
between finite beings, an addition by Marcel which characterizes the
philosophy of most theistic existentialists. Marcel has attempted to
reduce the tendency toward abstraction and empiricism in general
philosophy.

b. Existentialism in Germany has been represented by Karl
Jaspers (1883-   ) and Martin Heidegger (1889-   ) who have as
little in common as is possible for two thinkers who belong in the
same philosophical camp. More recently both of these thinkers have
refused to be called existentialists and have criticized the tendency to
crystallize and structure the tenets of this new mode of thought.

(1) Jaspers, the most influential thinker of modern Germany
was a professor of philosophy at the University of Basel in Switzerland
His knowledge of science and psychiatry has made possible his unique
contribution. To him, true philosophy and science are not opposite

to each other at all. Man and his existence are simply most fundamental. Jaspers should not be classed as either theistic or atheistic
although he discusses belief in God, the fallacy of determinism, and
agrees with Marcel in regard to the factor of communication between
selves. Like other existentialists, Jaspers disclaims absolute truth and
favors the independence of individual man. In his later years, he has
become increasingly interested in religion and inclined toward theism.

(2) Martin Heidegger, a student of Edmund Husserl (1959-
1938), the phenomenologist, provided the link between German and
French existentialism. He was also a professor of philosophy, at Frei-
burg, where he served in 1933 as rector. The early education of
Heidegger was in the scholastic tradition which harmonized with his
former commitment to Roman Catholicism, His writings are numerous,
and the best known is entitled *Being and Time*, (1927) and remains
unfinished. Heidegger has been a student of the philosophy of existence
and being. His fine distinctions have brought the unfair charge of
unnecessary obtrusiveness. In reality he deserves considerable credit
for focusing attention on the imperative need for man to accept both
the fact of his existence and the responsibility for self-development.

4. Jean-Paul Sartre (1905-)

Sartre is a French playwright, philosopher, and former university
professor. Because of his great importance at a period a little later than
that of Marcel, Sartre is given separate treatment here. He was born
in Paris, orphaned early in life, and brought up in a mixture of Protes-
tantism and Catholicism. Early in childhood he began to write brief
dramatic pieces. Later, he studied in Paris, and like Heidegger he
heard Husserl's lectures on phenomenology at the University of Göttingen. He became a schoolmaster, but in 1929 found himself con-
scripted into the French army. The Germans made him a prisoner,
but because of his delicate health, released him. His condition must
have greatly improved since he soon became a leader in the French
Resistance Movement, and as a result produced his *L'Etre et le Néant*
(Being and Nothingness, 1944). This writing and others which followed
were all motivated by his experiences in the French underground
where he came into daily contact with death, responsibility for others,
and the demand for liberty and freedom. Sartre has travelled abroad

several times since World War II, and twice he won the Nobel Peace Prize for Literature, once in 1945, and again in 1964 when he refused to accept it. Although less active now, Sartre is probably the best known existentialist of this century, and regardless of one's estimate of his contribution, he cannot be quickly dismissed.

Sartre, like Heidegger, is regarded as an atheist. Since God does not exist and the past is dead, man is very much alone, responsible only to create himself by his own acts. From his position of atheism, Sartre moves to a consideration of existence. His now famous aphorism, "Existence precedes essence," simply means that man is nothing except what he makes of himself by his free choices. Choosing is the one act he cannot choose to avoid. Man's essence is formed by his choices, not by universals. This situation confers an awesome responsibility upon each individual both for himself and for the image of man in general.

5. Some Other Contributors

A treatment of even most of the major contributors to this new approach to philosophy is both unnecessary and impossible in this case. Here are some of the thinkers not previously mentioned who might interest the reader:

Theologians such as Paul Tillich (1886-1965), who was active in the United States, Karl Barth (1886-1968), and Reinhold Niebuhr (1892-   ) are of note here. The religious philosopher Martin Buber (1878-1965) is another contributor. There is also Nicholas Berdyaev (1874-1948), a Russian Orthodox thinker whose philosophical position altered greatly throughout his lifetime, but who at least is remembered for defending the Christians in the Soviet Union before his expulsion from that country. The names of Albert Camus (ka-mu, 1913-1960), the French writer, and of the Spanish philosopher-statesman José Ortega y Gasset (1883-1955) are listed by some authorities as existentialists.

6. Present Status of Existentialism

Little attention was paid to Kierkegaard during his lifetime. But other factors were developing which would eventually change that.

There was the relentless search of experimental science for objective truth. That search produced the death-dealing weapons employed in the two world wars and in lesser conflicts around the globe. Science has not built for man the Utopia some leaders had promised. Instead, the horrors and conflicts of modern existence have been magnified by the discovery of atomic weapons of frightening power.

Most thinkers in the first half of the twentieth century viewed existentialism only as one of the consequences of the great world wars, and reasoned that it would soon go away. But for some reason this new philosophy behaved like a persistent soldier who kept firing not knowing the war was over.

Some youths in France asserted that they were existentialists and occupied an area on the left bank of the Seine. Called Beatniks by others, they utilized the new philosophy for their own purposes but refused to accept the tenet of responsibility. So, existentialism for a time implied that which was foolish and extreme. In any event, it was supposed to be a fad that would eventually fade into its own nothingness.

Instead of a transient existence, existentialism has grown in popularity. It reached the shores of the North American continent about 1946-1947, and has been busily making converts ever since. Its effects on the American climate of thought, on the society including the educational institutions, may not be measurable but neither can they be ignored. Many current students of this new mode of thought now profess to have discovered existentialist fragments in the Biblical stories of Abraham, Job, and Jeremiah. Some see existentialism in the ancient Greek tragedies such as those by Aeschylus and Euripides, in the life of Abelard, and more recently in *Brothers Karamozov* and *Notes from Underground* by the Russian novelist, Dostoevski. Current and leading proponents of this, our newest philosophy, are listed in the bibliography. The reader should give special attention to those named as contributors to educational existentialism.

B. PHILOSOPHICAL POSITION

Existentialism, both by its very nature and through its historical proponents, has resisted every attempt to organize its principles into neat and tidy categories. This aversion to systematic structure was the major factor in the renouncing of the label of existentialism by two of its best-known supporters, Heidegger and Jaspers. At the same time, the lack of an organized and logical presentation of its position has made this new mode of thought most difficult for students to understand. Its abstractness, coupled with extreme subjectivity, has retarded its promulgation, added to the criticism, and contributed to the wide range of positions and interpretations which now characterize the entire movement.

For the benefit of those readers who are new to the field of philosophy in general, and to existentialism in particular, an attempt has been made here to present the fundamental tenets according to the schema employed by classical philosophy.

1. Metaphysics

The nearest approach, offered by existentialists to the question of "What is real?" is the doctrine of existence. This consideration is prior to all others, constitutes the "first principle," and gives credence to the label, existentialism. Sartre's aphorism, "Existence precedes essence," means simply that the concept of existence is the proper starting place for philosophy. To exist is to presume an act by which one is; that is, an individual existent has appeared on the scene. At the moment of appearance that individual is characterized by that solitary condition of existence. This is not something man possesses; he is existence and nothingness.

Greek thinkers during the seventh and sixth centuries, B.C., the cosmological period, determined the historic direction of classical philosophy by their initial choice to search for the basic "stuff" of the universe. They, thus, sought for essence, not existence. Their answers ranged from objective particulars such as water, air, earth, fire, and even atoms, through the indefinable "boundless indefinite" to basic principles involving numbers and constant change. The fact that these thinkers could never agree on essence, and the consequent rise of skepticism, lends strength to the charge that perhaps these early philosopher-scientists failed because they were in error at the base. Existentialism would agree and insist that the first consideration is not essence, although that is significant; it is existence.

The existentialist's concept of existence is more than a simple recognition of the act of being. There is an appreciation of existence which is not to be automatically assumed. Many people apparently spend their entire lives without developing any deep understanding of personal identity. So, in addition to giving assent to the act of existing, one must bring about an acute awareness of personal existence. It might even be that there is a specific moment in the life of each youth when he suddenly becomes "existentially aware." Thereafter he must intensify that awareness.

2. *Epistemology*

It has already been stated that existentialism is adverse to the logico-epistemological structure of classical philosophy with its systematization and demand for reason. Knowledge obtained by an objective approach can be at best only hypothetical. Even knowledge arising from scientific methods is little better, and the fact that the pronouncements of the scientists are constantly being altered indicates that these so-called truths are mere approximations.

True knowledge, states the typical existentialist, originates with the individual. It arises from one's feelings and by intuition; it is human in nature. One does not discover knowledge; rather, each man chooses his truths as he selects the style and conduct of his life. For all of this he is responsible to himself. The validity of assumed knowledge cannot be measured by universals, since there are none, but by its value to its human chooser.

3. *Axiology*

Existentialist axiology has to do with certain aspects that are second only to that of existence. They are subjectivity with freedom and choice, essence and responsibility, in that order.

a. *Freedom and Choice*

Every consideration begins with the individual person. This subjectivity of existentialism can be readily seen in the emphasis upon the existent who states simply, "I exist." Although the act of existence is solitary and implies nothingness, it also make possible freedom and choice. In fact, according to Sartre, man has, or is, freedom in an absolute sense. It follows that since man does exist, and nothing else, and for that reason is free that he must choose and necessarily wills to do so. The only choice man is not free to make is the decision not to choose. He is not bound by other men, by society, or by any conditions external to himself. This principle rules out universals and determinism entirely.

Modern man, say the existentialists, has surrendered his freedom to the crowd, to society at large, and to dehumanizing technology. Our machines have not liberated us; they have enslaved us. Evil arises from following these tendencies. Man may fulfill himself only by renouncing the seemingly more stable, and also more crowded, world and facing the perilous task of knowing himself, his present and future. He is condemned to make such choices and to make them alone.

b. *Essence*

At this point the aspect of essence, so basic to the classical philosophies, assumes its proper place. Man is, and then he chooses. His choices both determine his own essence and contribute to the general view of man. What man chooses is value to him. All values arise from these free and wilful acts of individual man and not from abstract speculations. The human existent by his choices creates value and validates his own concepts of beauty and ethics.

c. *Responsibility*

Man, however, is responsible for his acts. He is not free to refuse to choose, but having chosen, he is free to fail by that act. It would be impossible to accept freedom without total responsibility or responsibility without absolute freedom. Whatever ensues, the individual man alone is guilty—never the situation, the society, or the crowd.

4. *Further Aspects of Existentialism*

Many of the most important considerations of this new mode of thought are not easily related chronologically to the areas defined by classical philosophy. They are treated here and in an order which, hopefully, is developmental in spite of the resistance of existentialism to logical structure.

a. *The Existential Being—Forlorn, Anxious, and Free*

John Donne said, "No man is an island . . ." which points to a position diametrically opposite of that held by the existentialists. A key word among proponents of this new mode of thought is forlornness. Theistic existentialists, such as Jaspers and Marcel who believe in communication between God and man, and between man and man, do not accept complete forlornness as do atheistic existentialists. Forlornness is, nevertheless, a basic tenet.

The existential being is forlorn in the sense that he is alone in facing every aspect of his existence. He is alone in the initial act of existing, its recognition, and in the process of intensifying his awareness of that act. Likewise he is alone in his decisions and in their effects. He alone is responsible for what happens to him. The existential man is alien to all other beings and to the meaningless universe around him.

Not only is man's existence characterized by forlornness. He is also intimately acquainted with anxiety. The development of awareness requires anguish and rises from a sense of dread. Such deep feelings of despair are the true guides to truth. These all-pervasive elements of existence are thus necessary and worthwhile—they are the "stuff" from which true philosophy spontaneously flows.

The causes of such feelings are several. A deep awareness of existence accompanied by absolute freedom of choice is a fundamental source. Added to this is the fact of personal and awful responsibility for one's own choices. Then there is the universe in which all this takes place, one that is neither hostile nor friendly; without any essence or meaning it can only be indifferent to man, and thus contributes to his suffering, his tension, his anxiety.

b. *The Paradox and the Human Predicament*

Here are two closely related concepts. The paradox which contributes to man's tensions is formed by the contrast between the nature of his existence and that of his universe. As soon as man becomes aware of personal being he also recognizes the possibility of non-existence. Man, unlike other creatures, knows he must die. The awareness of existence is fundamental and prior to all else, and yet man cannot have one without the other. Existence and non-existence are inseparable. As one existentialist stated, it is like the doughnut and the hole; no hole, no doughnut. Each man will eventually be erased, forgotten, non-existent. He, who is essence, succumbs to the essenceless, indifferent, alien universe.

The human predicament is a situation based on the belief that since nothing is predetermined, then there is nothing which makes human existence necessary. Existentialists point to the great wars and human tragedies which mark the history of that thin veil we call civilization. There have been great conflicts, poverty, epidemics, and mass killing almost from the beginning of time. Now science has discovered atomic energy and directed that power to even greater destruction, especially of human life. Man at heart is savage. Tillich adds that he is innately depraved, and this accounts for the evil treatment by men of men. This human predicament contributes to man's anguish, frustration, guilt, and despair.

c. Affirmation and Authenticity

The question which arises naturally at this point is simply, "What can man do about his situation?" Existentialism has a positive and challenging answer.

It must be assumed that the convert to existentialism has chosen to accept the aforementioned tenets, even if with considerable variation. He has recognized his own act of existence and intensified the awareness of personal identity. Further, he has exerted his freedom to choose and to select his values and thus determine his own essence. Also, he has recognized the paradox and the consequent human predicament as well as having endured the forlornness, anxiety, and anguish from which true philosophy emanates.

Now, man should assert himself, declare his personal value, and affirm the essence which he is. He should summon forth the best of himself, face the irrevocable paradox, the awful predicament, and the prospect of nothingness. This is an "encounter with life" in which man refuses to be defeated and engulfed by the human situation. In effect, this affirmation evidences an essence which does not deserve to be obliterated by a dumb and essenceless universe.

The consequence of man's affirmation does nothing to alter the predicament itself, but such a commitment makes the man an authentic individual. He still stands alone, is not of the crowd, but his encounter and acceptance of human dilemma has made him a true existent, an authentic person, something which none of the sciences could ever discover.

5. Existentialism and Pragmatism

Students are often quick to point out what appears to be obvious similarities between existentialism and pragmatism. However, most of these so-called similarities are superficial and emerge as underlying differences when pursued to some depth.

Neither existentialism nor pragmatism recognizes the existence of universals, and both disregard that metaphysical concept because it leads to determinism. But when pragmatism rejects universals it moves toward particulars which in turn lead to experimentalism and to the behavioral and objective sciences. Existentialism's repudiation of universals leads to human freedom and absolute subjectivity. What appears at first to be a common position becomes as opposing as that of matter versus man.

Similarly, these two schools agree that it is important in philosophy to consider human experiences. But it should be pointed that, whereas pragmatism places the continuum of experience, not the man himself, in a fundamental and metaphysical position, existentialism holds that there are prior considerations, such as human choice and existence itself. Dewey's self is biological while Sartre's is the inner man.

Pragmatism and existentialism are not as compatible in the field of epistemology as may first appear. They agree that speculation, especially that of Hegelian idealism, is unproductive of truth. But pragmatism utilizes considerable logic, and in spite of itself, some of the system-building approach to arrive at concrete data. Pragmatism sees truth as a quality which man creates as a consequence of experimentation and application. For the existentialists, truth simply arises from human choice and is purely subjective and absolutely relative.

Values, like truth, are chosen individually by the existentialist, while they are generated by both personal and social experiences, according to the pragmatist. Both emphasize doing as more important than knowing but even here there is the inevitable contrast between the utilitarian and the subjective.

6. *Existentialism and Other Fields*

This new mode of thought has been severely criticized for its subjectivity at a time when Western civilization has become extremely objective. The fact that some proponents are religious fundamentalists and others avowed atheists, indicating the absence of a common faith, is often noted, too. In addition, there are the problems of interpretation and comprehension which appear when one attempts to study existentialist literature, and the unpleasant and frequent reminder of anguish, dread, and death. Notwithstanding, as a climate of thought, existentialism has not only gained many supporters, especially among the younger generation, but it has also affected to some degree almost every other field of study. Some observors maintain that this new mode of thought has precipitated some very definite trends in the fine arts, which area has always been sensitive to philosophical changes with the artists themselves often unaware of the philosophy which motivated them to create their innovations. The most common examples given are impressionism in music and abstraction in art and painting. Meanwhile, psychology has attempted to counteract the effects of John Watson's behaviorism with the development of sensitivity groups, and with non-directive techniques in counseling, known now as client-centered therapy, and promoted mainly by Carl Rogers. Religion, too, has realized that man is involved in a contemporary dilemma and has become enmeshed in one itself. The current movement to disregard the historic dogmas of the church, especially its ethical precepts, and to let every man believe what he will, may be further evidence of the effect of what is often the unnamed philosophy, but recognized more and more as an expression of existentialism. The same spirit is seen in education in the trend toward individualized instruction, the equal value and vote of every student, and the challenging of every postulate of the total establishment. Western civilization is rapidly proceeding further and further away from the fixed standards of the puritan ethic to the subjectivity of existential freedom.

C. EXISTENTIALISM'S EFFECTS ON EDUCATION

1. The General Position

The question has often been asked, "Is an existentialist philosophy of education possible?" Negative answers may be the result of a limited view of the nature of philosophy. Although philosophical concepts are grouped for academic purposes into schools, theories, and movements, they rarely operate directly on the institutions of society and never in straight lines. Philosophy should not be thought of as referring to a shelf of frozen packages of logic from which one may choose. Rather, the various philosophies may be compared to the many tributaries which contribute to the gentle flow of a mighty river.

There does not seem to be an existentialist philosophy of education which can be deduced and separated from its parent. Such an organized presentation would be out of harmony with the movement. But when philosophy is viewed as a flow of ideas which gradually alters the educational climate, then there must be some underlying directives which can be identified. These concepts are as follows:

a. Human personality, subjective and individual, is the only proper foundation for education.

b. The emphasis should be on real existence, including freedom, choice, consequent essence, and the human situation.

c. The goals of education must be expressed in terms of awareness, acceptance, personal responsibility, eventual commitment and affirmation.

2. The Teacher's Role

An existentialist teacher is an initiator. He must necessarily instruct in the fundamentals, but beyond that he should direct his energies toward originating individual activities in which the student may or may not choose to participate. The course requirements and regulations on conduct would be kept at a minimum and coupled with a simplified approach to enforcement. Freedom should characterize the entire program since learning is private and personal. The teacher's task is to arouse the student to an awareness of his existence, which must then be intensified. Further, the teacher should promote the acceptance of freedom of choice and of responsibility for one's decisions. In effect, the opportunity to learn would be made available on a voluntary basis with the student largely responsible for his own program. The total environment would be altered, not to serve the administration, or the faculty, or even society, but the needs of the learner.

3. *The Student's Role*

If the teacher is the initiator, the student is the selector. The student decides what he will study and how much he will learn. If the teacher's task has been well done, the student will base his preferences on his personal and felt needs for self-identity, essence, and authenticity. He would be a free personality, not an imitator of his teachers, and never a follower of the crowd. Standards of academic achievement and of personal conduct would be chosen by the individual. Freedom for inquiry, interaction, and a sense of equality would characterize the student's relationship to his teachers.

4. *The Instructional Program*

Two closely related aspects must be dealt with here. First, there is the question of "What methods would be employed?" Second, there must be an answer to "What would be the content of the curriculum in a learning institution which was strongly existentialist?"

a. *The Method of Instruction*

The method of instruction would necessarily allow for a maximum of self-expression and choice. There might well be no formal instruction at all. Instead, every student in keeping with his own needs would pursue whatever areas of learning appealed to him. He would be initially involved in a search for himself and that task must not be interrupted by teacher intervention. Individualized instruction utilizing the student and his inner self, not teaching machines, would be important.

Whenever the teacher deemed it necessary to meet students in groups, the number involved at any one time would be few. In place of the standard formal lecture, the teacher would offer a number of discussion questions to which the students would be encouraged to respond. Under no circumstances would the instructor present ready-made answers, promote his own beliefs, or attempt to indoctrinate.

The Socratic method has often been given as a model for the existentialist teacher. True, the question-discussion approach of this method is existentialist in nature. But it must be remembered that Socrates always had his own preconceived definitions and answers, and his remarks simply directed the student to a point of agreement with the master. Such a method may or may not be typically existentialist, depending on the degree of directiveness by the teacher and whether the so-called truths are thought through afresh by every individual learner.

b. *The Curriculum*

The real curriculum, according to the existentialist teacher, is not found in the textbooks, or in the instructor's guides prepared by appointed committees in various school districts. Neither is it "what the teacher does after he closes his classroom door," as one educator stated. For the real curriculum is that which is in the mind of each individual student—not in the minds of certain supervising officials. That content to which the student addresses himself and which he voluntarily chooses to learn constitutes the actual curriculum. This is not the same thing as the instructional program which is proposed by the administration. Serious conflicts arise when the school officials are intensely traditional or classical and a number of the students are inclined to a modern version of existentialism.

The existentialist curriculum planner would offer the student opportunities to determine his personal identity, to have an encounter with life with all of its anxieties, and to choose for essence and authenticity. Such goals as happiness, security, and social adjustment would be incompatible in this program.

In keeping with these principles, it is consistent to assume that the humanities would occupy a paramount position. Contact with man's writings would expose the student to the realities of human tragedy, decision, and death. The interpretations of the literature would always be the student's own. And teachers would never lead the learner to a position where his understanding would be impeded by a morass of objective detail. The field of history and related social studies would have similar value and be taught in keeping with the same precautions against particulars.

The fine arts would receive more attention in an existentialist classroom than is currently the case in most schools. This would be especially true of drama. The composing and performing by students of plays and stories would assume a central place in the school program. Similarly, painting in all of its forms and music of every type would be presented by the teacher. The student's participation would always be in terms of his own choices so that he is free to be creative, spontaneous and individualistic.

In similar manner, play and physical activities would rank high in value. As in drama and music, the student is free to do what his inner self seems to require. He can abandon himself to personal expression and free choice in every movement.

One other, and quite different type of learning would be employed to achieve the goals of an existentialist classroom, namely, that of clear but abstract thinking and commitment, involving studies in religion, especially comparative, and philosophical. The content in these fields is personal, and belief eventually is found to be based on one's subjective decision—not on vague systems of logic. At the root of all ideas which man accepts are certain unprovable assumptions to which he has given assent. Both religion and philosophy should be discussed at every grade level, and the students urged to find their way to a deep and vital commitment. There is little freedom in no belief at all, while choice does not restrict one's freedom when the decision is personal and individual. The real evils in religion and philosophy are due to the use of forced learning, indoctrination, through creeds and catechisms, on one hand, and pure rationalism on the other.

Mathematics and the physical sciences would be of minor importance to the purely existentialist teacher. Both are aloof from man, impersonal, and like the universe to which they belong are indifferent to man's real needs. Their objectivity prevents any consideration of human feelings and reduces man himself to a mere thing. Both the effects on man and on the environment of scientism are evil. The study should not be promoted in the classroom.

5. Relationship to Society

For a theory, especially from the field of education, to be acceptable today it must have something to say about social betterment. But existentialism regards the individual as necessarily forlorn and the crowd as evil. This position makes the presentation of an organized program of social improvement almost impossible. Existentialism, thus, has offered no plan which specifically promotes the good society.

Existentialism does propose that each individual make his own choices which in turn determine his essence. It holds that each person is responsible for himself and for the general image of man. Perhaps this emphasis on personal choice and individual responsibility is the best and shortest, if not the only, route to a better society.

If existentialism has charted no particular course for societal improvement, its spirit has at least precipitated the founding of a number of educational institutions which have more in common with this philosophy than with any other. The Summerhill School, founded by A. S. Neill in 1921 at Leiston, Suffolk, England, is the best example. In typical existentialist fashion vague theory is scorned at Summerhill while freedom and choice with personal responsibility are given full play. Academic regulations are few in number and imposed mainly by outside authorities. Likewise, rules of conduct, requirements on attire, and other social conventions are almost non-existent. It appears, in spite of all the faults which the critics have pointed out, that the students at Summerhill enjoy a wholesome relationship with the members of the staff and with each other.

The Summerhill concept, sometimes called the Neillian view of education, has received widespread publicity. The English Summerhill Society was the first group to be formed. In 1961 the New York Summerhill Society was organized. The latter currently lists nearly 50 non-public schools in the United States which ascribe to the Neillian view. The Summerhill Society of Los Angeles was founded in 1968. The latter operates under some affiliation with the organization in New York. All of the preceding groups hold that the idea of freedom to learn requires also the freedom to be one's self, to determine one's identity, and to choose one's own future.

D. EVALUATION AND CRITICISM

Most of the commentary on the philosophy of existentialism and its accompanying educational theory and practice stems from the fundamental tenet of extreme subjectivity. There are both negative and positive opinions, of course, and usually the various objections or appreciations overlap. Here an attempt has been made to group the criticisms in large categories as follows:

1. Nature of the Philosophy

There is no philosophical position as subjective as existentialism. But this subjectivity often makes the philosophy more abstract than the classical theories and vague generalizations against which it is reacting. Further, the demand for subjectivity has rendered systemization of its position almost impossible and made comprehension of its principles extremely difficult. One has to almost accept and believe in order to understand and appreciate.

Also, the subjective nature of existentialism has multiplied the number of interpretations, yielded some inconsistencies and as many variations as there are exponents. Perhaps this is the price philosophy must pay if it is to encounter real truth.

2. Relation to Western Civilization

This hemisphere evidences certain trends which on the surface appear to be existentialistic. For example, we are freedom-loving and individualistic. But we are also preoccupied with pleasure, not grief, and hope, not despair. The people of the North American continent in particular differ extremely from those of either France or Germany after World War II. And now, even those countries, the cradles of existentialism, are more and more concerned with security, prosperity, and human happiness. Although existentialism has made a contribution to modern man through its recognition of the importance of human emotions, and its exaltation of personality, Western man is still primarily objective. He generally reacts negatively to a philosophy which refuses to consider any degree of scientific verification. We are an affluent, optimistic, and empirically-minded society.

3. Social Theory

The subjectivity of existentialism makes for a degree of personal freedom which would be intolerable on the contemporary scene. The same tenet seems to rule out any generally accepted value system so that social concern is without basis or motivation. In fact, it is true that existentialism does not even ascribe to a common religion, so typical of most schools of thought. With no principle other than that of subjectivity, social theory would be non-existent, and an organized institution of education as we now have would be impossible. Education under existentialism would not cease, but its nature would be drastically altered. Perhaps every student would simply "Do his own thing."

4. Strengths of Existentialism

If the weaknesses of existentialism arise from its position of subjectivity, so does its strengths. The emphasis on individuality, self-improvement, and personal involvement might as well do more for man and his society than any philosophy known throughout history. Every man must project his own solution to the human dilemma. For any number of men to agree to one answer would be to create a postulate and reduce every man's subjectivity.

FURTHER READING

Berdyaev, Nicolai. *Christian Existentialism* (trans. by Donald A. Lowrie). New York: Harper and Row, Publishers, 1965.

Bowers, C. A. "Existentialism and Educational Theory," *Educational Theory*. Vol. XV, No. 3 (July, 1965), pp. 222-229.

Dupuis, Adrian M. and Robert Nordberg. *Philosophy and Education*. Milwaukee, Wisconsin: The Bruce Publishing Company, 1964.

Dupuis, Adrian M. *Philosophy of Education in Historical Perspective.* Chicago: Rand McNally and Company, 1966.

Grene, Marjorie. *Introduction to Existentialism.* Chicago: The University of Chicago Press, 1948.

Harper, Ralph. *Existentialism, a Theory of Man.* Cambridge, Massachusetts: Harvard University Press, 1948.

Keohane, Mary. "A. S. Neill: Latter-Day Dewey?" *The Elementary School Journal.* Vol. 70, No. 8 (May, 1970), pp. 401-410.

Kneller, George F. *Existentialism and Education.* New York: John Wiley and Sons, Inc., 1958.

Morris, Van Cleve. *Existentialism in Education.* New York: Harper and Row, Publishers, 1966.

Morris, Van Cleve. "An Overview: Existentialism and Education," *Educational Theory.* Vol. 4, No. 4 (October, 1954), pp. 247-258.

Naess, Arne (trans.). *Four Modern Philosophers.* Chicago: The University of Chicago Press, 1965.

Nash, Paul, Andreas M. Kazamias, and Henry J. Parkinson. *The Educated Man.* New York: John Wiley and Sons, Inc., 1965.

Neill, A. S. *Freedom Not License!* New York: Hart Publishing Company, 1966.

Neill, A. S. *Summerhill.* New York: Hart Publishing Company, 1960.

Sanborn, Patricia F. *Existentialism.* New York: Pegasus, 1968.

Sartre, Jean-Paul. *Existentialism and Human Emotions.* New York: Philosophical Library, Inc., 1957.

INDEX

A

Abelard, Peter, 58, 65, 103
Adler, Mortimer, 62
Aeschylus, 103
Aesthetics, 8, 14, 20
Affective Domain, 6
Affirmation in Existentialist Philosophy, 108-109
Aims of Education in Classical Realism, 63
American Education Fellowship, 33
American Federation of Teachers, 70
American Spelling Book, 22
Analytic Statements, 86
Analyticism, 10
Andronicus of Rhodes, 10
Anthropology, 92
a priori, 35
Aquinas, Thomas, 10, 11, 58, 62, 63, 64, 100
Aristotle, 1, 9, 10, 11, 56-59, 62, 63
Arts, Fine
    In Existentialism, 114
    In Pragmatism, 38
    In Realism, 60
Atheism; Atheistic, 99, 101, 107
Athens, 56
Atlantic City, New Jersey, 50
Atomic Proposition, 84
Augustine, Saint, 21
Authenticity in Existentialist Philosophy, 108-109
Axiology
    General, 11-12
    In Analyticism, 90
    In Education, 14
    In Existentialism, 105
    In Idealism, 48

    In Pragmatism, 37-38, 41
    In Puritanism, 19-20
    In Realism, 60
    In Social Reconstructionism, 72
Ayer, Alfred Jules, 87

B

Babylonia, 56
Bacon, Francis, 33, 59
Bagley, William Chandler, 33, 50
Barr, Stringfellow, 62
Barth, Karl, 102
Basel, University of, 100
Beatniks, 103
Being and Time, 101
Berdyaev, Nicholas, 102
Bestor, Arthur, 24, 25
Bible, the; Biblical, 19, 20, 22, 103
Bode, Boyd H., 70
Boston University, 70
Bradley, Francis Herbert, 81, 82
Brameld, Theodore, 70, 71, 74, 75
Brickman, William W., 51
Buber, Martin, 102
Butler, J. Donald, 51

C

Calculus, 80
California, University of, 25, 86
Calvinism; Calvinistic, 18, 35, 95
Cambridge Group, 81
Cambridge University, 81, 82, 83, 85, 87
Camus, Albert, 102
Carnap, Rudolph, 85, 86, 87, 89
Catholicism; Roman Catholic Church, 63, 100

Chicago, University of, 32, 45, 62
Childs, John L., 70
Christian Religion, 97
Church of England, 17
Clarification, 91
Columbia University, 32, 62, 70
Comte, Auguste, 80-81, 88
Conant, James Bryant, 51
Conceptualization, 52
Conditions of Knowledge, 88
Conservative View, 45
Cook County Normal School, 32
Copenhagen, University of, 99
Cosmological Period; Cosmology, 8, 56, 104
Council for Basic Education, 25
Council of Trent, 58
Counts, George S., 70
Cultural Heritage, 53
Cultural Lag, 53
Cultural Reality, 71
Curriculum
    Of Analyticism, 93
    Of Essentialism, 52
    Of Existentialism, 113-115
    Of Reconstructionism, 74-75
    Of Traditionalism, 22, 23

D

Dark Ages, the, 61
Darwin, Charles S.; Darwinism, 23, 42
Demiaschkevich, Michael, 50
Democracy; Democratic, 38, 52, 66
Depraved; Depravity, 19, 108
Descartes, René, 10, 80
Determinism; Predestination, 18, 106
Dewey, John, 1, 12, 26, 29, 32, 33, 35-36, 40, 69, 109
Discipline, Puritan, 21
Donne, John, 107
Dostoevski, 103

E

Eclectic; Eclecticism, 3, 64
Economics, 92
Edwards, Jonathan, 18
Egypt, 56
Einstein, Albert, 85
Either-Or, 99
Eliot, Charles, 32
Emerson, Ralph Waldo, 23, 47
Empiricism, 59, 86

Encounter in Existential Philosophy, 108-109
Ends and Means, 36, 37, 57
Epistemology
    General, 10-11
    In Analyticism, 90
    In Existentialism, 105
    In Idealism, 48
    In Pragmatism, 37
    In Puritanism, 19
    In Social Reconstructionism, 71-72
Erasmus, 61
Erskine, John, 62
Essence, 104, 106
Essentialists, 33
Essentialist's Committee for the Advancement of Education, The, 50, 53
Ethics, 8, 14, 37-38
Euripides, 103
Evolution, 36, 42
Existentialism, 5, 9, 10
    Contrast with Pragmatism, 109
Experience; Experiential; Experientialism, 29, 35, 36
Experimentalists; Experimentalism, 29, 35

F

Faculty Psychology, 25
Fadiman, Clifton, 24, 25
Formalism, 17
Foundations of Education, 92
Franklin, Benjamin, 34
French Revolution, the, 98
Froebelian Principles, 32
Frontier Thinkers, 70
Fuller, Professor, 45

G

Gasset, José Ortega y, 102
Geometry, 80
George Peabody College, 50
God
    In Analyticism, 90, 95
    In Aquinas, 58
    In Existentialism, 98, 99, 100, 102, 107
    In Puritanism, 18-19, 23
    In Realism, 60, 65
Golden Mean, the, 57
Göttingen, University of, 101

Great Books Foundation, the, 62
Great Depression, the, 50
Greek Philosophers; Philosophy, 1, 8,
    30, 35, 45, 56

H

Harris, William T., 50
Harvard University, 32, 34, 51, 83, 88
Hegel, Georg Friedrich, 10, 47, 98,
    109
Heidegger, Martin, 100, 101, 104
Heraclitus, 36
Herbart, Johann Friedrick, 1, 50
Howick, William H., 50 (footnote)
Human Predicament in Existential
    Philosophy, 107-108
Husserl, Edmund, 101
Hutchins, Robert Maynard, 62, 64
Hylomorphism, 58

I

Idealism, 9, 45-49
India, 56
Industrial Revolution, 34, 81
Innate Ideas, 39
Instrumental; Instrumentalism, 29, 35

J

James, William, 35
Jaspers, Karl, 100, 101, 104, 107
Jefferson, Thomas, 34
Johns Hopkins University, 34
Judd, Charles H., 32

K

Kandel, Isaac L., 50
Kant, Immanuel, 1, 10, 46-47, 86
Kierkegaard, Soren, 98-99
Kilpatrick, William Heard, 69
Königsberg, Germany, University of,
    47

L

Language Analysis, 87
Language Games, 84
Leibniz, Gottfried Wilhelm von, 47,
    80
L'Etre et le Néant, 101
Linguistic Analysis, 88-90

Locke, John, 1, 10, 22, 34, 39, 49, 59,
    80
Logic
    Deductive, 14
    General, 10-11
    In Aristotle, 57
    In Education, 13-14
    In Idealism, 48
    In Pragmatism, 37
    Inductive, 14
    Methodologies, 11
Logical Atomism; Logical Empiricists;
    Logical Positivists, 83, 85, 88, 89

M

Mann, Horace, 31
Marcel, Gabriel, 100, 101, 107
Maritain, Jacques, 62
Meade, George H., 35
Mental Discipline, 64, 67
Merchant-Taylors' School, 61
Metaphysics
    Dewey's View, 35
    General, 9-10
    In Analyticism, 90
    In Aristotle, 57-58
    In Education, 13
    In Existentialism, 104
    In Idealism, 48
    In Pragmatism, 36-37
    In Progressivism, 40-41
    In Puritanism, 18-19
    In Realism, 59-60
Methods
    In Analyticism, 93
    In Essentialism, 52
    In Existentialism, 112-113
    In Puritanism, 21-22
    In Traditionalism, 24-25
Michigan, University of, 88
Milesians; Miletus, 7, 56, 79
Mill, John Stuart, 35, 82
Milton, John, 59, 61-62
Mind, Concept of, 36-37, 41
Moore, George E., 81, 82, 83, 87, 89
Montaigne, Michael de, 61
Mulcaster, Richard, 61
Music, 57, 110, 114

N

Natural Punishment; Naturalism,
    30-31

Nazi Party, 85
Neef, Joseph, 31
Neill, A. S., 115
Neo-Experimentalists, 71
Neo-Scholasticism, 55
Neo-Thomism, 55, 59, 60, 67
New England Primer, 22
New Harmony, Indiana, 31
New York, College of the City of, 82
New York Times, 33
Newman, John Henry Cardinal, 62
Niebuhr, Reinhold, 102
Nietzsche, Friedrich Wilhelm, 99-100
Nobel Peace Prize, 102
Nominalism, 65

O

Ockham, 59
Ontology, 9
Oxford University, 83, 87, 89

P

Paine, Thomas, 34
Paradox in Existentialist Philosophy, the, 107-108
Paris, the University of, 58
Parker, Francis Wayland, 31-32
Parmenides, 80
Pedagogic Party, the, 70
Peirce, Charles Sanders, 34-35
Perennial; Perennialism, 55, 60, 61-66
Pestalozzi, Johann Heinrich, 31, 47
Phenomenology; Phenomenologist, 101
Philosopher Kings, 65
Philosophical Investigations, 84, 89
Philosophy
    And Education, 12-15
    Approach, 6-8
    Critical, 7-8
    Defined, 7
    Divisions, 9-12
    Prescriptive, 7-8
    Speculative, 7-8
    Values of, 8-9
Pilgrims; Puritanism, 17-22
Plato, 1, 11, 46, 49, 56, 57, 58, 65
Political; Politics, 5, 73, 76, 92
Positivism, 64, 79
Pragmatism; Pragmatists, 4, 9, 64, 65, 86

Progressive Education Association, 32-33
    Periodical of, 32
Progressivism, 4, 5, 45
Psalter, the, 20, 22
Psychology; Psychological, 11, 12, 24, 25, 39, 92, 110
Pythagoreans, the, 79-80

Q

Quincy, Massachusetts, 31
Quine, Willard Van, 88
Quintilian, 30

R

Rabelais, 61
Rationalism, 99
Realism, 9, 55-60
Reflective Thinking, 72
Responsibility in Existentialist Philosophy, 106
Rickover, G. Hyman, 25, 40
Rogers, Carl, 110
Roosevelt, Theodore, 23
Roscellinus, 58
Rousseau, Jean Jacques, 30-31
Royce, Josiah, 47
Russell, Bertrand, 81-83, 87, 88, 89
Russell, Lord John, 82
Ryle, Gilbert, 87
Ryle, Walter H., 50

S

Saint John's College, 62
Saint Louis, Missouri, 50
Saint Paul's School, 61
Sartre, Jean-Paul, 101-102, 104, 106, 109
Scheffler, Israel, 88
Schlick, Moritz, 85, 87, 89
Scholastics, 58
School Administration, 74
Schools of Thought, 4, 6, 7
Sciences
    Behavioral, 77
    Physical, 23, 24, 34, 65, 73, 114-115
Scientific
    Approach, 9
    Principles, 8
    View, 6

Separatists, 17
Seven Liberal Arts, the, 62, 64
Shane, Milton L., 50
Shaw, F. Alden, 50
Shores, Louis, 50
Skeptics, 11
Social Consensus, 72, 76
Socialism, 76
Social Philosophy
    Of Analyticists, 94
    Of Classical Realists, 65-66
    Of Essentialists, 52-53
    Of Existentialists, 115, 117
    Of Progressivists, 40
    Of Puritanism, 18
    Of Social Reconstructionists, 72,
      73
Social Self-realization, 72, 73, 76
Sociology, 12, 77, 92
Socrates, 46, 56
    Method of, 113
Soviet Union, 102
Spanish American War, 23
Sputnik, Russian, 51
Stevenson, Charles Leslie, 88
Story of the Eight-Year Study, The,
    42 (footnote)
Student's Role
    In Analyticism, 93
    In Essentialism, 51-52
    In Existentialism, 112
    In Progressivism, 39
Subjective, Subjectivity, in
    Existentialism, 98, 105-106
Summerhill School, 115
Summerhill Society, English, 115
Summerhill Society, New York, 115
Summerhill Society of Los Angeles,
    115
Syllogism, 11, 14, 57, 60
Synthetic Proposition, 86

T

Teacher's Role
    In Analyticism, 92-93
    In Classical Realism, 64-65
    In Essentialism, 51
    In Existentialism, 111-112
    In Progressivism, 39
Technology, 5, 59, 106

Teleological, 57
Thales, 56
Thoreau, Henry David, 23
Tillich, Paul, 102, 108
Tractatus Logico-Philosophicus,
    83-84, 86, 89
Traditionalism, 45
Truth
    General, 11
    In Analyticism, 90-91
    In Existentialism, 105
    In Idealism, 48
    In Pragmatism, 37
    In Progressivism, 41
    In Realism, 60, 66
    In Reconstructionism, 72

U

Ulich, Robert, 50
Universals, 9, 46, 57-58, 106, 109
Unmoved Mover, The, 58, 65
Utilitarian; Utilitarianism, 23, 35, 79,
    81, 82

V

Values, 12, 60, 110
Verifiability; Verification, Principle of,
    86
Vienna Circle, the, 85-86, 88-89
Vienna, University of, 85
Virtue, 60

W

Waismann, Friedrich, 85
Watson, John, 110
Webster, Noah, 22
Whipple, Guy M., 50
Whitehead, Alfred North, 82-83
Wisdom, John, 83, 87
Wittgenstein, Ludwig, 83-85, 86, 87,
    88
Woodring, Paul, 33
World Wars, 17, 50, 100

Y

Yale University, 62